CALLED to a LIVING HOPE

Inspiring Stories of Faith

CALLED to a LIVING HOPE

Inspiring Stories of Faith

Jan Edith Taylor

Rekindle Publishing

Athens Georgia

Called to a Living Hope

Use of Scriptural Quotations of the Holy Bible

Scripture quotations, unless otherwise identified, are from the Holy Bible New International Version copyrighted from The International Bible Society. NKJV is the abbreviation for the New King James Version, by Thomas Nelson, Inc. KJV is the abbreviation for the King James Version, RSV is the Revised Standard Version, NRSV is New Revised Standard Version and the Amplified Bible is also used. None of the quotations exceeds the allowed number of quotations by these publishers.

Printed in the United States of America

Paperback ISBN: 978-0-9988619-7-5
ePub ISBN: 978-0-9988619-9-9

Rekindle Publishing
1711 Meriweather Dr., Ste 104
Watkinsville, GA 30677

"Be of good courage, And He shall strengthen your heart,
All you who hope in the Lord."

—Psalm 31:24 NKJ

May these stories bring God's presence to you.
Jean Edith Taylor
(Mark 4:30-32)

Contents

Acknowledgments

While writing my first book, *Heritage of Hope: Lives Touched by God's Transforming Power,* I was awed to meet people with beautiful stories of faith. Now for this second book, *Called to a Living Hope*, I was certain God had plans to introduce me to people with amazing stories once again, and I was not disappointed. Thank you, storytellers, for trusting me with the publication of your testimonies.

Dorothy Trout Slaga was an enthusiastic supporter of this collection. She introduced me to people in Virginia who had been part of her mother's Thursday Night Prayer Group, as well as other Christian friends. Dorothy, thank you for allowing me to use excerpts from the journals of your mother, Lucile Wilson Trout.

When I started this second book, I knew I needed a group of authors who would critique my writing. Lindsey Sanford opportunely started a Writers Group at the Lenawee District Library in Adrian, Michigan. INK members have been faithful to provide me with kindly encouragement and thoughtful critiques. Thank you so much, especially those of you who have continued to read the stories for the entire eight years of the project. Thank you also to Rick Bonfim Ministries for guidance in the publishing process.

The completion of a project such as this is dependent on intercessory prayer. I am appreciative for faithful prayer partners in the Brooklyn Presbyterian Prayer Committee, St. Rita Catholic Prayer Group, Third Thursday Ecumenical Prayer Group, my four Virginia Sisters who have prayed for me and my family since the 1970s, and my Prayer Partner of many years, Rev. Susan Kingsley. As I came close to publication, I felt the need of someone to specifically pray for the successful completion of this project. My new friend in our Women's Sunday School Class, Ann Johnston, offered to pray for me and did faithfully. Thank you, Ann.

Finally, speaking words of encouragement to me for fifty-seven years is my husband, Ed. As the pandemic made it difficult to connect with those who could edit the final copies, Ed faithfully read and re-read everything I wrote and gave me insightful critiques and corrections. Thank you, Ed. Thank you also to my son, Bill, and his wife, Julie, and grandsons, August and Clay. Your constant love and support are always precious gifts. Gratitude also to faithful friends and readers who have read my books and passed them on to others. My prayer is that you will enjoy and find hope in reading this latest collection.

Thank you, Father, for the witness You give of Yourself in each story. Thank You for guiding and helping me. To You belongs all the glory.

Introduction

One bitter Michigan winter afternoon our Church's Christian Education Director, Betty Blue, and I met at church talking about plans for Vacation Bible School. As we visited, Betty began to tell me about her childhood and the challenges she and her husband had faced as adoptive parents of boys taken from abusive home situations. As she expressed the faith that brought her through her difficulties, I knew I had the first story for a second book. Betty had a philosophy of life that took her through many trials. Not only did she survive, but her solid faith and positive viewpoint enriched the lives of all those around her. Betty died suddenly in December of 2019, and we all miss her. Hopefully the publication of her story will continue her legacy of assuring others of God's love.

Betty's story is just one of nineteen contained in this second book, Called to a Living Hope. The stories come from a variety of situations where people are called to demonstrate their faith in God. I know you will be inspired by their courage, and the grace and mercy of God demonstrated in their lives.

As I am putting the finishing touches on this publication, there is a pandemic sweeping across the world. Sitting in front of our television sets, we see pictures of downtown areas across the world, silently shuttered with no traffic moving on broad boulevards. My mother-in-law at ninety-nine is puzzled to be confined to her room in an assisted living facility where we can only visit from her porch and talk through the sliding glass door. We shop for groceries with masks covering our nose and mouth, unable to see the expressions of our neighbors as we move down one-way aisles. My own church is limited to small numbers, socially distanced for in-person worship. We wait for the discovery and release of cures and vaccines. A variety of tests, which will advise us of contagion or health, seem too few to meet the worldwide demand. Some people have antibodies that protect them, but no one knows how long that immunity will last.

I thank God for the Scriptures that encourage me each morning, especially Romans 8:28 that says that God will use everything, even a pandemic, for good for those who love Him. One of my favorite passages in Genesis is the story of Joseph who in chapter 45:5,7 tells his brothers that what they meant for evil, God is using to preserve their lives. God *is* in control. Romans 5:3-5 gives us cause to rejoice in our sufferings. "...because we know that suffering produces perseverance; perseverance, character; and character, hope. And hope does not disappoint us, because God has poured out His love into our hearts by the Holy Spirit, whom He has given us."

It has taken me eight years to collect and edit the stories presented in this book, and they *are* stories of hope. When Covid-19 struck and we were all confined to our homes, I was in the final stages of collecting all the stories needed for publication. It was the perfect time to begin the process of finishing the manuscript. As the world darkened, I was amazed at God's perfect timing.

For some of you, the story-tellers are beloved people who have crossed your path, but in their honest accounts, you will discover fresh wisdom to overcome struggles, and answers to prayer. For every reader, I pray you will find healing, hope, and encouragement.

May these testimonies lift up Jesus, who brings us a living hope: that in His death we have forgiveness, and in His resurrection an inheritance of strength for today and the promise of everlasting love (1 Peter 1:3,4). All praise to Him.

1

God Is Faithful! – Norma Jean Nelson

"Never will I leave you; never will I forsake you." God's pledge in Hebrews 13:5b became the touchstone upon which Norma Jean Nelson relied when her husband of ten years asked her for a divorce. "Although I was emotionally devastated, I determined that this would not devastate my life," the petite, vivacious fifty-seven-year-old mother of twin boys recalls. I had two precious boys to raise, and they needed their mom. I knew God would never leave me. I chose to stay close to the Lord—that's what got me through—leaning on God and trusting Him. I determined that I would put my energy into raising my sons to be men of God. I decided they were more important than my own selfish desires; I didn't pursue a relationship. I focused on Joey and Davey."

"I made the decision to never speak negatively to my boys about their dad. He was always invited and included in whatever the boys did." She set her heart on making sure her sons did not have the baggage of bitterness and anger towards their father.

"I wanted them to love him—because he would always be their dad." She says that to this day, now in their 20's, they love their dad and he loves them.

The boys' father was faithful to take his sons on visitation days and vacation, but they lived with their mom. He helped with expenses but Norma Jean increasingly paid the majority of the bills. Norma Jean was a stay-at-home Mom who home-schooled the boys until fifth grade. Her livelihood was from her cake baking business, an occupation she had pursued from age sixteen. *"God is faithful!"* Norma Jean emphasizes. "My bills were never late. God was faithful in every area of my life."

After six years of separation, her husband decided to make the divorce final on December sixth. As Christmas approached, Norma Jean was again facing many uncertainties, especially regarding financial provision for herself and her sons. Her in-laws continued to want a close relationship with her and the boys, and that year, as in the past, they were invited to celebrate the holiday with them. When she and the boys returned home Christmas Eve, they spied a package on the porch! Norma Jean looked inside the gift bag to discover a pair of leather gloves and a long, beautiful coat in red, her favorite color. Later, she learned that some friends had gone together to buy the coat and gloves. "Whenever I wear that coat, it reminds me of God's faithfulness to care for me," she says. Meanwhile, cake orders came in just when needed.

Since the twins lived with Norma Jean, she was the one to discipline them, to make sure their homework was done, and to faithfully take them to church on Sundays and Wednesdays. She struggled sometimes with being the parent with those kinds of responsibilities, while the boys' father was the "fun dad." Nevertheless, Norma Jean was firm in supplying the structure she knew was best for her sons.

When Joey and Davey were in seventh and eighth grade, they rebelled against some of the rules of the house. "Why do we have to go to church?" they would ask. "*Dad* doesn't go to church."

Norma Jean was not swayed. "You don't live with your dad. You live here, and *we* go to church."

Their resistance ended when, as sophomores in high school, they went on a mission trip to Bolivia. Norma Jean recalls, "That was a life-changing experience for them—to realize that not everyone has all the things Americans have, and yet people who were so poor shared the little they had." Many mission trips followed that first one, and the boys' desire to take the Gospel to others was born. Today both of Norma Jean's sons are licensed ministers. Davey just returned from serving as a missionary in Ghana, West Africa.

Norma Jean's health had been the least of her concerns until, in October of 2012 at age fifty-seven, Norma Jean began to bleed in a manner she suspected was abnormal. When the bleeding continued for three weeks, she made an appointment to see her gynecologist. A biopsy brought a diagnosis of hyperpiesia of the uterus, a pre-cancerous condition.

Norma Jean comes from a large family and there had been many incidences of cancer. Her gynecologist ordered tests and all of the results came back negative. Nevertheless, he gave her three options, to do nothing and keep an eye on it, to have an ablation, or to have a hysterectomy. She chose to have a hysterectomy. She reasoned, "If you take the uterus out, then it can't get cancer."

At church Norma Jean had been studying the book, The Circle Maker by Mark Batterson. Following the author's recommendations, she decided to make her time of recovery from surgery a time of worship and prayer, a period of seeking God, to draw closer to Him. During this time, Norma Jean had the impression that God was doing something new in her life. "I was open to whatever it was," she says. She was told there would be a recovery of four to six weeks, but a week and a half later she was able to be back to her job as Church Secretary.

With no pain whatsoever and feeling fit, Norma Jean went for her check-up and the results of the pathology report. A friend had given her a devotional for Christmas, Jesus Calling by Sarah Young. The day before her doctor's appointment on January 25th the reading encouraged her: *"Let my love enfold you in the radiance of My Glory. ...Through the intimacy of our relationship, you are being transformed from the inside out. As you keep your focus on Me, I form you into the one I desire you to be. Your part is to yield to My creative work in you, neither resisting it nor trying to speed it up... Hold My hand in childlike trust, and the way before you will open up step by step."*

The Scriptures in *2 Corinthians 3:18 and Psalm 73: 23 – 24* reinforced this message. Also, she encouraged herself by remembering the promise in Hebrews 13: 5b – *"Never will I leave you; never will I forsake you."*

At her doctor's appointment, Norma Jean's gynecologist told her he was shocked that the pathology report revealed she had uterine cancer. All the tests previous to the surgery had been negative and when he operated, he saw no sign of cancer. Therefore, he had confidently performed a routine hysterectomy, and had not taken any lymph nodes for analysis. He apologized to her because now her medical team could not be sure they had removed all the cancer. "I have already made an appointment with a gynecologic oncologist," he told her soberly. She would need to have radiation and/or chemotherapy.

He had treated her for over twenty-five years and knew her well. She was a quiet person, who never talked much about herself or her life. But Norma Jean began that day to experience a *new boldness* to share her faith—with him and with others.

When he told her not to worry about the treatments, Norma Jean assured him, "I don't worry. God is bigger than cancer." The doctor was quiet.

"How could the cancer not have shown up in the biopsy that was done prior to the surgery?" Norma Jean wondered aloud. The doctor explained that the biopsy had been done on the lining of the uterus, but the cancer was in the muscle itself.

The reading for that day, January 26th, in Jesus Calling said: *"Give up the illusion that you deserve a problem-free life. Part of you is still hungering for the resolution of all difficulties. This is a false hope! As I told my disciples, in the world you will have trouble. Link your hope not to problem solving in this life but to the promise of an eternity of problem-free life in heaven. Instead of seeking perfection in this fallen world, pour your energy into seeking Me: the Perfect One. It is possible to enjoy Me and glorify Me in the midst of adverse circumstances... I am much less interested in right circumstances than in right responses to whatever comes your way."*

The scriptural references for the day emphasized the same message: John 16:33 and also: *Psalm 112:4,7 "Even in darkness light dawns for the upright, for the gracious and compassionate and righteous man. He will have no fear of bad news; his heart is steadfast, trusting in the Lord."*

After Norma's surgery, her sister called. "How are you feeling?" she asked.

Norma gave the answer she was giving to everyone, "I have some discomfort from the surgery but no pain."

The next question caught Norma off-guard, "What did the doctor say?"

"I have cancer." Norma's sister began to cry. Norma assured her sister that God had healed her. "They removed the cancer even though they didn't know it was there but God knew."

By the end of the conversation Norma's sister laughed and said, "I wanted to comfort you, but you have comforted me."

Her prayers in the days prior to her oncology appointment were: "God, whatever brings you the most glory, is what I want in my life. I just ask you to radiate Your love in my life to everyone I meet."

Norma Jean also asked her pastors to pray and anoint her with oil. She told them how grateful she was that the surgeon removed the uterus without knowing the cancer was there. She was also heartened that the cancer was stage one; usually uterine cancer is not discovered until it is stage three or four.

Because she was not dismayed by this news, she shared it with Joey and Davey in an up-beat spirit, assuring them God had already healed her because the uterus had been removed. Joey seemed to take the news in stride. Norma Jean did not realize how traumatized Davey was until she got a call from his supervisor in Ghana where Davey was serving as a youth pastor. "Davey wants to know if he should come home to be with you," the man explained. "He is worried." Norma called Davey again and explained in more detail why she felt that the cancer was no longer there, and that by no means should he travel from Ghana to be with her. She promised to keep him up-to-date about everything involved in her treatment. He seemed more at peace.

At her appointment with the medical oncologist, a PET-Scan, a chest x-ray, and blood tests were ordered. In the days that followed she met with the oncology radiologist to learn about procedures for chemotherapy and radiation treatments. The entire month of February was taken up with tests. On February 25th she had an appointment for a dry-run on what would happen when her treatments began.

Meanwhile, Norma Jean was asking, "God, why do I have to go through treatments if you have already healed me?" Always she stayed true to her resolve, "But whatever brings you the most glory is what I want."

On her second visit to the oncologist, she learned that all the results for her tests were completely normal and negative for cancer. As a result, she would not need to have chemotherapy but she *would* need to proceed with radiation treatments. The oncologist specialist, the medical oncologist, and the radiation oncologist all recommended radiation therapy since surgical procedures were not followed for cancer removal.

Having heard the recommendations of the medical team, Norma Jean struggled to understand what *God* wanted her to do. If she went through treatment, did this show a lack of faith? After all, God had told her she was healed. Before she went for her first radiation treatment, she decided to follow the guidance of Proverbs 11:14, to seek the advice of multiple counselors. She sought out direction from three mature Christian friends, including a medical doctor and a minister. The medical doctor told her, "There is nothing wrong with taking advantage of the wisdom, knowledge, skills, and technology that God has given doctors."

"Even though I feel God has already healed me?" Norma Jean asked.

He countered, *"Let the doctors be the ones to say it is a miracle."*

"Okay God," Norma Jean prayed, "I'm taking this as wisdom from you."

Yet, at her first treatment she felt constrained to ask the radiologist, "Why do I need to go through this? Why? All my test results are negative for the presence of cancer." He explained that sometimes microscopic cancerous cells are not detected by tests. Radiation would assure them that all cancer had been destroyed.

Facing radiology every day, Monday through Friday for twenty-eight treatments, she prayed again, "God, whatever brings you the most glory is what I want. Shine your love through me into the lives of others." She also prayed that the side effects would be minimal, and God answered both prayers.

"I am a baker," Norma Jean says, "and I love to share what I bake. I also make greeting cards, mostly from pictures I have taken." When she went in for her hysterectomy, she made individual bags of cookies and a package of cards for everyone involved with her surgery. She gave gift bags to the friend who went with her to the hospital, to offer to the people behind the scenes that she would never see. "I wanted them to know how much I appreciated what they were doing for me," she said. "This was before I knew I had cancer."

With the new diagnosis Norma Jean began to bake cookies and package cards to give to the eighteen members of the staff involved in her radiation treatments. She also wanted to encourage the cancer patients who came into the waiting room before and after her each day. As she waited in the lounge for her treatments, she would ask people their names. "People don't normally share any information about themselves in a waiting room, but I like to know people's names," she says. She brought them gifts: sometimes cookies, other times cards, flowers from her garden, and seeds. She told a patient eighty years old that he was the same age her dad would have been if he were still alive. "In honor of my dad," she told him, "I have made you some cookies."

One day this elderly gentleman said, "Let me ask you: You're the happiest person I've seen here and yet you have been diagnosed with cancer. How can you be so joyful when you have cancer?"

With confidence, Norma Jean answered, "I don't have to be afraid. Jesus Christ is the same yesterday and today and forever (Hebrews 13:8). He goes before me; He goes behind me; And He walks beside me, holding my right hand. My joy comes from Him and knowing He's walking through this with me. Jesus gives me peace and joy." She paused, "And God has already healed me. They took the cancer out before they even knew it was there."

"You'd better put an extra offering in the collection plate," he said, shaking his head in wonder.

One of the cancer patients was a young construction worker. Norma Jean asked him, "How are you doing?"

"I am blessed and highly favored," he answered with a warm smile. When he came back from his treatment, she asked him if he was a believer in Jesus? "Yes, I am," he told her. He shared with her that the way God was helping him through this time of battling cancer was just astounding. He had leukemia and had been in remission but now the disease was back.

Norma Jean brought pumpkin muffins to a woman fighting stage four cervical cancer. She had four children and was discouraged. Norma Jean befriended her and stayed in touch, supporting her through four surgeries.

"I really want to stay in touch with you after you finish your treatments," an older woman told Norma Jean. "There aren't many people who cross our path like you." The next day the woman brought dinner to Norma Jean. Norma Jean understood the sacrifice the woman made in making the meal.

"People who are taking chemo and radiation may have neuropathy in their hands and/or feet. She had it in both and for her to do this for me was a special gift," Norma Jean says.

The patients asked Norma Jean if her baking was a business. She told them truthfully that, yes, she baked for a business. "You should bring in some business cards," they told her.

"You know what, I didn't bring my baked goods to promote my business," Norma Jean explained. "I brought them to bring encouragement."

Once a week Norma Jean had "doctor day," when she would see her radiation oncologist. On March 12th, his nurse handed her the consent papers for HDR (High Dose Radiation) Brachytherapy, the internal radiation treatment for the targeted area. "Take these home, read and sign them, and bring them back," she told her. Norma Jean decided to put action with her faith and to completely trust God for direction and take Him at His word. She was convinced God had already healed her and she didn't need any further treatment. She communicated this to the nurse. "The doctor wants you to do this. You really need to do this," the nurse emphasized.

For the next Doctor Day her regular oncologist was on vacation. After treatment the radiation technologist mentioned that her HDR treatments were scheduled to start the following week. Norma Jean said that she had already advised her doctor of her decision not to have any further treatments. The technician was annoyed with her. "You are going to have to go to the nurse's station and work this out because your doctor is going to want you to do this." Norma Jean was relieved when the nurse simply said she should wait until the following week to talk to her oncologist.

"Inside I was still wrestling." She confesses. I wondered, "Am I making the right decision? God, I need to *know* that I'm making the right choice."

Her devotional reading for that day seemed an answer to her prayer. It was a Bible story of Jesus healing two blind men who had called out to Him (Matthew 9:27, 28). Jesus asked the men "Do you believe that I am able to do this?" As she read those words, Norma Jean knew that this was also what Jesus was asking her, *"Do you believe I can do this for you?"*

She answered, "God, I *do* believe you can do this." She would repeat this over and over to herself as an affirmation of her faith.

Then, the enemy would come in with the thought, "What if the cancer comes back?"

Norma Jean reminded herself, "God holds all of my days in His hands." She had a choice to make: fear or faith. *"I chose faith,"* she says.

Meanwhile, it was her elderly friend's last treatment day. To celebrate she took him some homemade apple sauce and cookies. He told her, "I can see Jesus in your eyes, hear Him in your voice, and see Him on your face." His job was that of an undertaker, so he went on to tell her, "I've met other people who say they are Christians, but their walk doesn't match their talk."

Without having heard the old man's words, the construction worker told her the same: "I can hear Jesus in your voice; I can see Him in your eyes and on your face."

As her own treatments were drawing to an end, Norma Jean wanted to do something special for her doctor. Three weeks before she had asked his nurse to tell her which cookies were his favorite, and learned his favorites were Girl Scout Samoas. She went on-line to find the recipe. It was a complicated procedure in order to achieve the various layers, but on April 2nd she took a basketful for the doctor and a platter for the staff. Since she was headed for her treatment, she gave the cookies to his nurse. A few moments later, the nurse came back to where Norma Jean was waiting. "I wish you could have seen his expression," she told her. "His whole face lit up, and would you believe—today is his birthday and no one knew."

Norma Jean smiled to herself thinking, "*Jesus knew.*"

After her treatment, the nurse talked with Norma Jean, trying to change her mind about further therapy. Norma Jean explained again that she was not doing the HRD treatment because God had already healed her. She shared the message of Psalm 112:7, "I will have no fear of bad news; my heart is steadfast, trusting in the Lord." Norma Jean told the nurse that her treatment had been a pleasant experience and she believed her purpose in coming to the treatment center was to bring encouragement.

"You have certainly done that," the nurse told her. "Everyone will miss you."

Since this was her Doctor Day, she also saw the oncologist. After a short chat thanking her for the cookies, he confronted her about the decision not to proceed with the HRD treatment. He told her that she really needed to continue and do the internal radiation, because if the cancer were to return her quality of life would decline precipitously.

She told him how much she appreciated all that he had done for her and the other cancer patients. She asked him not to be offended by her decision. Earlier he had referred to her "religious beliefs." Now she explained, "It's not a religion, it's a relationship. I trust in the Lord and He has healed me." Again, as she had done with others, she personalized the message of Psalm 112: 7, telling him she had no fear of bad news because she was trusting in the Lord. She told she believed the Bible, God's Word to be true. "God has given me peace and joy and I don't have to be afraid." She expressed to him her belief that God gives doctors abilities, skills, and technology to bring hope and healing to people. Again, she thanked him. "I am grateful that God uses doctors; *however,* God has healed me, so I don't need the HRD treatment." Then smiling up at him she said, "You're the best."

She got up to shake his hand, but he reached out and hugged her. "You are great," he told her.

As the day of her final treatment approached, Norma Jean wrote each of the eighteen staff members a personal note, thanking them for using their God-given talents, skills, and gifts to bring hope and healing to people with cancer. She included the blessing in Numbers

6:24,25. "The Lord bless you and keep you; the Lord make his face shine upon you and be gracious to you; the Lord turn his face toward you and give you peace." She included in each note the ABCs of Salvation and instructions for opening their hearts to Jesus.

She describes her last day of treatment: "On that day, after you are finished, cancer patients ring a bell three times at the nurses' station. The staff is usually busy seeing and attending to patients, but on my last day many of the staff gathered around me, and gave me numerous hugs." As she hugged one of the treatment therapists, Norma Jean said, "I wish I could tell you how much I love all of you."

"You have—you showed us," she told Norma Jean. The staff had signed a card thanking her for the goodies, flowers, and words of encouragement, her sunny disposition. Over and over she heard, "We are going to miss you. We don't often meet someone like you."

Norma Jean summarizes this experience as follows: "Meeting all the new people God brought across my path and building friendships with them made my treatment a pleasant experience. To God be the glory."

On July 21, 2013 Norma Jean went back for her six-month check-up. Her doctor told her that all of her medical team agreed she was cured of cancer.

"I have a personal relationship with The Healer," she says quietly at the end of her story, "and am grateful for the stripes He took on His back for my salvation and my healing (Isaiah 53:5).

2

A Light in the Darkness – Betty Blue

"I've had a wonderful Christian life," Betty Blue says with a twinkle in her eye. "My parents were interested in me and what I did, and wanted me to succeed."

Her earliest memories of life on the one hundred sixty-acre family farm in northern Iowa include the sweet aroma of spring borne on a gentle breeze, the sight of moist black soil freshly turned by the plow, and the peace of livestock grazing in the meadows. In her home there was the fragrance of home-baked bread, bouquets of vivid flowers in every room, and the sound of good music from her sister's piano: Bach, Beethoven, and Chopin. There was a large vegetable garden, and at harvest time, the pleasure of viewing fields full of golden grain as far as the eye could see.

"There was a freedom on the farm that people don't realize today," Betty elaborates. "We didn't worry about things beyond our family and community life. Growing up as I did, I didn't realize people could have such serious problems. It was a joyful time in my life.

I loved being a part of the farm, the kitchen, and then prayer at the end of the day. I am so grateful to my parents and grandparents and thankful for my heritage. My childhood, grounded in faith, was a preparation for the disappointments I faced in life. This early foundation prepared me to help others."

"My father was first generation Norwegian-American, a strong leader in the church, and well read. He was quiet, reserved, stately—and opinionated," she adds with a smile. Her mother, second generation German-American, was a great homemaker. "She not only had a garden and chickens, but she was a good cook." At Christmas her mother baked a delicious combination of Norwegian and German pastries. From her mother Betty inherited a love of beauty and color, and from both parents an ethic of hard work.

When Betty began to struggle with her third piano teacher, her older sister LaVonne, a gifted musician, offered to help. She sat on the piano bench beside Betty and, "through good times and bad," Betty says, "LaVonne made me practice faithfully forty-five minutes a day for a year." By the time the year was over, Betty could appreciate Mrs. Hodgeman's piano instruction. "My piano playing and love of music I attribute to my sister."

While she was in college, an ad in a Youth for Christ magazine alerted Betty that a man who tuned sleigh bells and cow bells, thirty-six in all, was wanting to sell his collection. The bells were valued at four dollars each. Betty was helping on the farm that summer and she told her father, "I will do anything you want me to do on the farm, if you will help me buy those bells."

One of the happiest moments in her life was the day her mother called her in from combining oats to tell her, "Betty Lou, your bells are here." There in the dining room were two boxes. Betty unwrapped each bell with excitement. There were no directions, but with her knowledge of piano, she soon had the thirty-six bells lined up according to their notes, and played her first song, *Jesus Loves Me**.

"That was one of the greatest afternoons of my life," she remembers. "I sat on the tractor in the oat field, thinking of all I could do with the bells. I planned to play bells with a team of young people—and I have done that. I thought, 'I will play in other churches—and I did that. I hoped I would travel with my bells throughout the United States—and I did. I wanted to travel to other countries to play the bells—and I did that, serving on mission teams and playing the bells as my contribution. I envisioned that I would someday play for the President of the United States." As this story was being written some church friends got together to make a video of Betty playing her bells, including a patriotic narrative she gave, interwoven with songs. The video was sent to the White House to Michelle Obama's staff who handled gifts and thank you notes. When she hadn't heard anything over the next year, someone asked Betty if she was disappointed. In her usual positive style Betty said, "Someone in the White House has heard me play the bells," and she seemed to enjoy that thought.

Betty's family was well-educated. Her mother's two brothers had their doctorate degrees and taught in colleges, one of them a professor at Asbury Seminary. In addition to these up-standing men, their gracious wives and her grandmother were an inspiration to Betty. "My family was strong in prayer," she says. "Daily devotions and prayer were an important part of each day, morning and evening." Betty attended a four-year college and graduated with an elementary education degree. Her love for children would become the hallmark of her life.

After she married, she and her husband adopted three boys: the first two were brothers and a third boy was welcomed later. The boys, seven, nine, and eleven years old at the time of their adoptions came from troubled families. "We knew this would not be an easy task, but we figured with love, reading and learning in a Christian home, the boys would eventually adjust. They were very active, and for three or four years everything went well." As the boys entered their teen years, however, the family began to fall apart. Betty's sons had major problems at home and at school. Their anger, disrespect, and foul language were foreign to her experience.

"My husband and I did all the things parents do in a situation like ours: we went to counseling; we tried to talk with our boys, but talking did not work," Betty admits. "The hardest thing was the rage and the disrespect. I did not know how to help my sons. Of course, I experienced anger about things from time to time, but their anger was beyond anything I had ever seen." Looking back, she believes her sons were deeply wounded by the fact that their birth parents let them go; they felt abandoned. They began to stay out late and used drugs. "I didn't want to tell other people about my problems with my boys. I felt like a failure."

Betty and her husband joined a group at their church for parents of middle school children who had been adopted. Betty received encouragement, sharing with parents living through similar problems in their own families. She faults social workers who are eager to place abused and troubled children in homes, but then do not follow through with counseling and help in the painful adjustments that follow. "Parents are not prepared, often times, to help the children they have grown to love," she says sadly.

Betty went on with her schooling to acquire a Master's Degree in Special Education. Her training and experience with schoolchildren with behavioral disorders helped her at home. It has also equipped her to counsel other parents with problems with their children through the years. Nevertheless, following four years of teaching Special Education, she returned to the regular classroom. "I was happier there. It was too traumatic dealing with serious behavioral problems at school all day and then come home to more of the same."

Finally, the boys graduated from high school, "by the grace of God," Betty exclaims! "Then they went out on their own." One son is occasionally in contact with her, but the other two sons have not been in contact with Betty for many years. Meanwhile, her marriage ended in divorce.

As the year 1978-1979 dawned Betty experienced some difficult losses. In November of the preceding year her sister was diagnosed with colon cancer, and lived only a short time. Then in August Betty's father died of a stroke and a cousin also died. Betty shares that in the sadness of mourning, and also when her mother died on Easter, she learned not to fear death, that death can be beautiful. "I felt God in my life at that time," she says. "When my time comes, I am not afraid. I know I will be with my family."

Her mother, the last of Betty's immediate family members to die, was concerned that now her daughter would be alone, without family. "I told her that I knew God would take care of me and I was okay with it. *'I love you, I love you, I love you!'* I told my mother. With that she took her last breath and was gone."

Amid all the struggles in her life Betty learned to cope by praying and turning to music. "Music soothes my soul." Hymns from her childhood resurfaced to bring healing. "*Great Is Thy Faithfulness*"* and "*It is Well with My Soul*"* are two of her favorites. When she is disturbed, she plays the bells, taking special pleasure in the bass tones of the large bells. "When I shake those big bells *hard*, it gets rid of my frustration," she confesses. "*When You Ring Those Golden Bells*"* is one rousing tune she especially delights in, shaking the lower-toned bells for all they are worth. "People enjoy it," she says with a grin.

Having learned the value of hard work on the farm, Betty finds that keeping busy and working in the church are antidotes to feeling sorry for herself. "I know how hard it can be," she says about families experiencing the problems of modern-day life. "I tell young couples that while their concern causes them to focus on their children's needs, they must also take care of their own needs."

She works today as Christian Education Director in her church and ministers to parents as well as children. "It helped me to know that people were praying for me when I was going through the hard times and now, I pray for others," she declares. She has seen miraculous answers to those prayers. "Two children with cancer are now in remission," she confides with quiet pleasure.

Betty also uses her musical gifts to brighten the lives of others. On a regular basis she visits nursing homes and assisted living complexes, playing the piano for the residents. She has a children's bell choir, and gives piano lessons.

Joan Thomas, a member of the church, works with Betty and observes her interaction with Joan's grandchildren when Betty gives them piano lessons. "Betty would never say or do anything to hurt a child's self-esteem," Joan explains. "She is a protector, and treats each child as if he or she were her own. She is a character builder. She has a musical gift to share and doesn't hold anything back."

Betty knows that certain children never practice. She might kid them a little bit, but she never scolds. She continues the lesson so that these children have, at least, that time of practice. When there are mistaken notes, she might say, "Our fingers are like people—some are strong and some not very strong." When beginners have difficulty playing with their left hand, she will talk about the hand as if it were a person: "That left hand certainly has a hard time," or "The left hand forgot to play!" Then, "This song reminds me of you—it is calm, the notes sound good together." In praise: "Oh, isn't that a beautiful sounding chord? You are the best! Great job!" If a child has a problem with a particular passage, she will play along with them, helping them get the hang of it, and then dropping off as their confidence builds. "I'll bet you couldn't tell who is playing," she will comment. "You're doing wonderful." And Joan says the truth is that often she cannot tell where Betty leaves off and the child continues to play, emulating his teacher.

"For recitals each child is assigned a piece that is challenging," Joan continues, "and almost no one plays perfectly. Betty is seated on the piano bench with all but the oldest students, and she quietly encourages, helping them find their place, and praising each one. They love their lessons and their teacher, and are eager to do more." Betty understands from her own experience that playing the piano gives children who are troubled, an activity which takes their mind off their worries. Music provides a creative outlet, giving them a sense of accomplishing something beautiful. Of her twenty-five students a few even receive lessons from a distance, over the telephone!

Thanksgiving this past year one of Betty's sons brought his friend and her son to visit with Betty for a week. It was a glorious week! At each meal Betty prayed, thanking God for the great day they had had. She learned later that her son was thrilled with these prayers and when he returned home, began to pray before meals. Her son told Betty that she had changed his life, and that his memories of her were good ones. Betty was encouraged to see that her son was building a good life for himself and those close to him. While he still may go long periods without responding to her cards and letters, suddenly there will be a Mother's Day card or note, or flowers for her birthday. Betty prays for all three of her sons to find peace. She has a close relationship with one of the ex-wives and her grandson and often visits them in Arizona. Betty also maintains contact with her sister LaVonne's children, and travels to spend time with them in Canada.

In addition to this family, Betty has the family she has formed with her caring ways. On her birthday this past May, Betty received gorgeous cards with many personal messages, thanking God for the day she was born, and celebrating the difference her presence has made in peoples' lives and the lives of their children.

Betty Blue smiles her calming smile.

Isaiah 54:1b,10 (NRSV) seems to fit this lovely woman's life: " ' For the children of the desolate woman will be more than the children of her that is married,' says the Lord. 'For the mountains may depart and the hills be removed, but my steadfast love shall not depart from you, and my covenant of peace shall not be removed,' says the Lord who has compassion on you." Betty Blue moved to Arizona in July of 2019 to live near her daughter-in-law and grandson. She passed away in December of 2019.

* *Jesus Loves Me* – Anna B. Warner and William B. Bradbury; *Great Is Thy Faithfulness* – Thomas O. Chisholm and William M. Runyan; *It Is Well with My Soul* – Horatio G. Spafford and Philip P. Bless; *When You Ring Those Golden Bells* – de Marbelle

3

Prayer for Woundedness

The following is a powerful prayer that can be prayed for the healing from a painful childhood. The person being prayed for does not need to be present.

"Prayer for Healing of Those Who Are Wounded"

– Author Unknown

Father, I pray for the innermost being of the tiny child inside ____________ (name of person you are praying for). Lord Jesus, I ask You to identify with the wounded spirit all the way back to the time of conception.

I say to you ______________________(name), in the name of Jesus, that your life is not a mistake. God made you out of the love that He is. He called you into being at the right time and the right place. He prepared a way for you and gave His life for you. You are a privilege, not a burden;

a joy and a delight, not a disappointment; you are not an intrusion, you belong. You are a treasure just because you are, not merely for what you can do. You are one of Father God's own children, and He delights in you, and I delight in you.

Lord Jesus, destroy whatever lies this child may have accepted, and I bring to the cross every resultant destructive attitude, expectation, and personality structure or habit pattern. I see you, Lord, pouring Your love into this child, breathing a fresh breath of life into his/her spirit, wrapping strong welcoming arms about her, and inviting her to grow into the fullness of her own life, restfully, as God planned for her from the beginning.

I pray that the inner child be enabled to forgive those who wounded him. I also pray that this child himself be forgiven for his negative responses. I pour the healing love of Jesus into the wounded spirit like a healing balm. Give this child a sovereign gift of trust and rest and peace, and cause his entire being to be integrated with wholeness and harmony as he is reconciled to being who he is, where he is.

I place the cross of Jesus Christ between this child and her parents and her parents' parents all the way back through the generations, declaring that all of her inheritance be filtered through that cross.

Dear God, hide this child in Your own heart and cast light into the eyes of any powers of darkness who might attempt to oppress, afflict, or prevent his life. I stand in the authority of Jesus Christ against such powers.

I place a blessing on this child in the name of Jesus Christ. Melt any hardness of heart, strengthen her with might in her inner man, enlighten the eyes of her heart, open doors for her, draw her to her destiny, and place a mantel of protection on her for her future life.

I pray this prayer to the Father, sending the power of the Holy Spirit forth to heal, in the powerful name of Jesus, God's Son. I believe, according to 1 John 5: 14 – 15, when my prayer is in the will of God, and when I believe God hears my prayer, then I ***have*** what I have prayed for. Thank you, Father God, for healing this child, whether slowly or immediately. To You be all the glory and praise and honor. Amen.

4

A Servant in Need of Rest – George and Mary Ashley

In the main court of the suburban mall, lines of people follow a snowy path leading to the platform where Santa Claus holds little ones on his lap. Grown-ups and children chatter over the strains of Christmas music as they breathe in scents of pine and cinnamon from candle shops. Gold and silver garlands drape doorways and arches. The brilliant colors of Christmas adorn shop windows, adding to the holiday mood. Amid the bustling crowds, parents and children wait patiently to see Santa Claus.

But this is not just *any* Santa. This Santa's face radiates love for each child who mounts the stairs. He is so popular, year after year, that children look forward to entrusting their Christmas wishes to this kindly man. When younger children are fearful on their first visit to Santa, crying and protesting as their parents urge them forward, Santa leans down to look into the child's face, speaking gently and quietly. Soon the cries are silenced and not only does the child curl up in Santa's lap, but often they keep coming back and resist their parents' efforts to leave.

Santa's real name is George Ashley and he considers his role as Santa Claus a divine calling: to help children understand the true meaning of Christmas.

When he dresses as Santa Claus, George wears a cross around his neck. He wants children to know that this Santa knows the Christ of Christmas. George says that sometimes a child will ask about his necklace. They might say, "What's this? What does it say?"

George will spell out the letters on the cross: "J-e-s-u-s. That spells Jesus." Some children have never heard that word before. George will explain, "Jesus is the name of the One whose birthday we celebrate on Christmas. Do you know Jesus?"

"Who is he?" the child may ask.

"Jesus is God's Son. God created the world and everything we see around us. Then, He sent His Son to show us how to live." Depending on the age of the child and his curiosity, George sometimes tells the story of Jesus' death on the cross and His resurrection. He tells children that they can pray for Jesus to come into their hearts and be their friend.

While George attended church with his family from childhood, his own journey to know Jesus as Friend and Savior was most influenced by his maternal grandmother. Blinded at a young age from diabetes, she enjoyed playing hymns on the pump organ, and instilled in her grandson a love of music. George remembers the two of them listening to Billy Graham give the invitation to receive Jesus as Savior on television, and her asking him, "Do you believe that?"

George answered, "Yes, I *do* believe that."

"You need to commit your life to the Lord," she insisted.

"I know," George answered. "I'm going to but I can't right now.

"Without the steadying influence of Christ in my life as a teenager," George says, "I did some really dumb things in high school while associating with the wrong crowd." His marriage to his wife Mary turned his life around. It was at their church in Goldvein, Virginia, that George was baptized. He says, "As I came up out of the water, I felt like a new person. My sins were all washed away; it was a glorious experience." George began to see the Lord's hand on every aspect of his life. He knew God was in control. "I wanted to do whatever the Lord wanted me to do."

George began his first stint as Santa Claus when he was sixteen years old. From the beginning George loved children. Years later when he and Mary learned that a father in their neighborhood had deserted his wife and three boys, George could not bear that Santa might not visit these children. The twins were almost three years old and the other boy an infant. George and Mary contacted the mother and she was delighted to allow Santa to deliver gifts she had purchased. George dressed up in his red suit and brought the gifts to the three children. This became a family tradition: every year Santa Claus appeared at the door with gifts for the boys. Meanwhile, George played his role as Santa Claus in shopping centers and malls in the area around his home. That is, every year but one. The Christmas of 2002 was a holiday George does not remember.

George had begun to have a series of health problems. He was a customer service representative, listening to people's complaints all day long. He was responsible for several telephone lines at once and so the pressure was constant. After an examination, his doctor recommended a leave of absence from work. He told George that unless he took time off, the results could be life threatening.

George was a conscientious employee. He feared he might lose his job if he took time off. On the other hand, he was looking forward to future grandchildren, so he took the doctor's advice and left his position for four weeks of rest. When it was time to return, George dutifully went to his desk. At times that day he spoke to his fellow employees and seemed completely normal, but at other times, as the insistent telephones rang, George stared off into space and did not respond.

"I don't remember anything about that day," George says. "Later they told me I was ordered to drive many miles to the office where the company doctor was located. How I did that without killing myself or someone else, I don't know except that God was watching over me."

The doctor could not find a physical problem and told George to return to work. Still oblivious to everything around him, George dutifully drove back, parking two blocks from his normal parking spot. Once again, he sat at his desk and stared into space. When quitting time arrived, George did not move. One of his friends insisted they call 911. The ambulance came and took George to the hospital.

At the hospital they examined him but no one could find anything wrong. Fortunately, they decided to keep him overnight for observation. A bed in a room at the end of the hall was assigned to him but an attentive nurse objected. "Put him in the room next to the nurses' station where I can keep an eye on him." Now George's symptoms escalated. He curled into a fetal position and shook violently. He had a number of seizures. By Friday of that week, he was not able to breathe on his own so they put him on a ventilator. At one point, George's heart stopped completely. This nurse's demand that he be put in close proximity to the nurses' station probably saved George's life.

Later, Mary sought to find the nurse to thank her. Armed with her name, the time and date of duty, Mary asked the hospital staff to locate her. She was told that no one by that name or matching that description worked for the hospital; neither could the staff recall such a person being on duty that night. George and Mary are convinced the nurse was an angel sent to watch over George.

Meanwhile, no one at the hospital was able to diagnose what was wrong with their patient. Mary and the two children decided to transfer George to another better-equipped hospital.

At the new hospital, George went into a coma-like state. Mary trusted God was healing her husband, keeping him safe from further trauma.

Everyone knew George loved music; he and Mary led worship in their small church, George singing and Mary playing the piano. Their son Robert refused to be discouraged by a lack of diagnosis. He told his mother and sister, "We have been taught to praise God in all things." He brought hymnals and his sister located a keyboard and everyone who came to the hospital would sing. The youth group came every day after school and when no one was there to sing, George's family played CDs of praise music in his room. In addition, the call for intercession went out to prayer ministries around the world.

After twenty-seven days in a coma, George awakened. The hospital staff immediately got him up to walk; they supported him, using a belt. Now that he was conscious and able to speak, Mary could see that the seizures and having to be resuscitated had caused damage to George's brain. George called her, "Darlene," and would tell strange tales about going to Annapolis. In addition, all the time in bed had caused great weakness; George had lost almost 100 pounds. The hospital declared him ready to return home, but although Mary tried her best to manage at home it was an impossible situation. She could not afford to miss work for fear of losing their only source of income. George was too weak to climb the stairs to their bedroom so they slept on a sofa bed downstairs. George would become disoriented and get up in the middle of the night while Mary slept. Twice he had fallen.

This turned out to be a blessing. Their doctor told Mary the next time George fell to call an ambulance and have him readmitted to the hospital. Insurance would kick-in and his care would be covered again. She followed his advice and George was able to re-enter the hospital.

When George was finally ready to leave the hospital for the last time, it was necessary for him to continue in therapy for three years. Mary's job was a blessing for the struggling family. At first, Robert drove his father to therapy. Then, Mary discovered that using her business address, she could take George to work and use transportation supplied by the county to take him to the hospital and return him to her office at the end of day. Again, using that address, they were able to take advantage of Speech, Physical, and Occupational therapies. These were expensive for Mary but key to George's recovery. As part of a special program for those with brain injuries, George worked in groups to practice buying groceries, managing money, and all aspects of daily life that he needed to re-learn. In time, George was able to live without help at home, although he still struggles to remember things.

During the years of George's illness and recovery, God provided for the Ashleys. They look back in wonder at the provision of Mary's job. Just before George's illness, the company for which Mary worked had gone out of business and although she searched diligently, Mary wasn't able to find a new job. In desperation, she had cried out to God and felt impressed to take a position at a temporary agency which eventually led to her current job. This position put her where she needed to be for transportation to George's therapy once he was released from the hospital.

God also strengthened Mary's faith whenever she faltered with just the right song or teaching. In December of 2002, shortly after George's admittance to the hospital, Mary listened to a teaching CD on trusting God. "Nothing is impossible with God," the speaker emphasized. Mary took hold of this message, listening to the CD over and over again. Returning one evening from the hospital where she had been told George could die at any moment, she wept as outside, the rain pounded her car. The words of a Gloria and Bill Gaither song came to mind and she sang over and over again: "Because He lives I can face tomorrow, Because He lives, all fear is gone; because I know He holds the future. And life is worth the living just because He lives."

God also provided financial support. After George began recovery therapies, the couple struggled with a crushing load of debt. One morning Mary decided to mail the mortgage payment even though she knew they were $245.00 short. In the mail that day a friend had, unsolicited, sent a check for $245.00, the exact amount needed. Other checks arrived from church members, just when necessary, and one couple paid for George and Mary to attend recreational trips sponsored by the church.

Mary did her best to arrange installment payments for the medical bills, but a hospital bill for $5000.00 had to be postponed. Over a period of several years when the hospital pressured her to pay, she explained their circumstances and promised to pay as soon as they were able. When that day came, she went into the offices, bill in hand. The clerk looked up the records and assured her that she no longer owed anything. The bill had been outstanding so long that it had been wiped from the records. Mary was overwhelmed with relief and gratitude to God!

Although George has not been able to find a job since his illness, he finds all kinds of ways to help others. He volunteers with hospice, checking on supplies with care-givers and filling out forms to ensure they get what they need. He can encourage them from his own experience: "Don't give up. You never know what God is going to do!" He loves rocking babies once a week at a near-by hospital. As he rocks, he prays for each little one.

And every summer George begins to grow his white beard in preparation for his role as Santa Claus.

At Christmas time in 2012, George was in for a surprise. The neighborhood family George and Mary had 'adopted,' appeared at the Ashleys' door; this time *they* brought gifts. Among the presents was a photo album showing pictures from all the Christmases the boys had celebrated with a personal visit from Santa. An additional blessing was that the youngest boy, now sixteen, was decked out in his own Santa Claus suit. He told George that from now on he would play Santa, wanting to pass on the blessing his benefactor had given him.

George came out of his struggles with some insights to share:

1. **"Don't let stress get to you!** I thought I was just tired. Looking back now, I can see what happened." Since his illness George has heard of people dying from too much stress. He says, "Stress is a serious problem; it can kill you. *Do everything you can to get relieved of it.*"

2. **"Stay close to the Lord; He will get you through, even when it seems impossible.** I mean, I had to have three years of speech therapy, and physical and occupational therapy."

There is an old hymn which says, "But I know whom I have believed, and am persuaded that he is able to keep that which I have committed unto him against that day."* George and Mary have trusted in Jesus all through their lives and found when trials came, indeed, *God is faithful.*

* This is the refrain of the hymn written by Major Daniel Webster Whittle with music by James McGranahan, taken from 2 Timothy 1:12 KJV.

George Ashley as Santa Claus gives praise and worships the Lord Jesus Christ at the creche at the Spiritual Support Care Ministry, Warrenton, Virginia.

5

A Changed Life – Annette Patterson's Story

Phil Patterson was an amazingly talented Heavy Equipment Mechanic. From his early training as a tool and die maker he was even able to make the tools he needed when they were not available. Anything that had to do with a mal-function at the concrete company where he worked, Phil was the one they counted on to fix it. But his life changed in a drastic way in 1983, when God miraculously saved his life.

His wife Annette's first clue that something catastrophic had happened came with a phone call from the plant. Her eldest son took the call: "Tell your mother that your dad got caught in the coal crusher and they can't find his heart medicine." Annette didn't totally understand the message but she knew it was not good. She learned later that Phil had been buried under twenty tons of coal.

The plant had a problem that day and was shut down while some of the workers left to get parts for the repair Phil was doing. One of the supervisors had failed to put a lock in place and as Phil stood on the coal to work on the crusher overhead, the coal shifted like quicksand and buried him alive.

When the workers returned with parts, they looked around but there was no sign of Phil. Then they heard him praying in the coal pile. As the coal sucked him under, his hardhat shifted miraculously giving him an air pocket making it possible for him to breathe—and to pray. It took them twenty-two minutes, digging feverishly from the bottom of the coal pile, to free him. He lost three inches of height from the pressure of the avalanche, and would have back problems the rest of his life, but Phil survived.

"I was really proud of how he changed his life after the accident," Annette says, her voice quiet but carrying conviction. "He re-dedicated his life to the Lord and was re-baptized."

Before the accident Phil would tell his family, "I paid for this with *my* money. Everything you have is because of me, I work a job and provide. "

Annette says it was true Phil was a hard worker; he had grown up on a farm where he did chores before school and after school. However, after the accident, when they bought their first house, Phil told her, "This isn't really our home. We are just allowed to live here. God's the One who has been providing all these years for our family. The sooner my children understand that the better off they'll be. You have to work a job, but God provides it for you."

As a result of being buried alive in the coal pile, Phil spent three years on disability, but finally his company forced him to return to work at a desk job. While it was difficult to return to work in the place where he almost died, he told himself he would use his new position to protect the workers. Anything that threatened the safety of his fellow workers Phil reported to the Occupational Safety and Health Administration (OSHA). He was aware that he could be fired, but he wanted to make sure that no one had to go through what he had experienced because of someone else's carelessness.

Phil's desire to understand the Bible became a consuming passion. Every day he read four versions of the Bible and he had a Bible sitting on his desk at work. He read Scripture to people who were having trouble, sharing his faith with them. Annette says, "I became accustomed to people dropping by our house to ask Phil to take a ride with them; they wanted to tell him about a problem and have him pray with them or tell them what Scripture said to do. He never talked about what people shared with him and they learned to trust him."

About this time Annette and Phil took on the responsibility of caring for Annette's dad who was in the hospital for gangrene of the bowel. When he developed blood clots, he was flown to the University Hospital. "When my dad was in intensive care, my husband prayed with a lot of people and a lot of miracles happened. Even for my dad. He had many panic attacks. They wanted to take him off the ventilator because the longer he was on it, they were afraid he might never get off. One night we just got home from visiting my dad when the hospital called to say, 'Your dad can't breathe. He's having a bad panic attack, and we can't seem to do anything about it.'

"My husband and I turned around and drove back to the hospital. The nurses watched as we each took dad's hands on either side of the bed and prayed and asked God to calm his breathing. We just talked to God in a conversational tone. Eventually the nurses that weren't doing anything came in and joined hands with us and prayed and after we were done, my dad was all calm."

"One of the nurses said, 'You know, we all got a good lesson here tonight. If that's what it takes to calm a person who is having a panic attack—anyone who is not working on a patient, we are all going to join hands and pray just like you did.' When we came back the next time, they told us they were actually able to do it!"

"My husband commented, 'We just need to trust *God*.' "

"When we were at the hospital, people would wait at the elevator for Phil to get there every day from work to pray for a family member." The doctors would not allow Phil to go into intensive care because of bringing germs, but he would pray over the family member requesting prayer, sometimes anointing them with oil.

One woman had been told by the doctor that her brother was near death and they needed to take him off the ventilator. She told Phil she could not accept that. "I want you to come down and pray for my brother."

"So we went down," Annette says. "Lots of people had gathered and we were all holding hands and praying for her brother to be able to breathe once they took him off the ventilator. The doctor called the man's sister to come back into the room with him. We didn't know if he had died or what.

"*It was marvelous.* Her brother had come around and was talking and knew everyone by name. The doctor was overwhelmed by it."

At one point the medical personnel, detecting bleeding in Annette's father's stomach, thought he had cancer. He was not doing well and the doctors said he had only minutes to live. Annette refused to take him off the ventilator and just let him die. She told Phil, "Dad gave me power of attorney and I promised to do whatever is needed to get him well. I'm also not going to believe it's cancer."

Phil said, "Let's go down to the hospital chapel and we'll pray." As he prayed in the chapel, Phil told her God spoke to him and told him that by midnight the blood in her dad's urine would be totally gone and there would not be any more bleeding.

"The doctor thought we were crazy," she says. "When they took his bag off at midnight and tested his urine, there was no blood in it." Later, the doctors realized the bleeding had been from ulcers.

"We felt rewarded every day we were there with my dad. I hated driving there in the winter, but when I walked in, he would make the sign of the cross and he was so happy." As he improved, Phil and Annette brought him home and he lived two more years, accomplishing everything on his bucket list, visiting family and friends.

Annette and Phil's faith was tested especially when on November 22, 2003 their eldest son, Phil Jr., was murdered. He had been working in Florida, transporting vehicles by semi-truck all over the country. The day of his death, the day before Thanksgiving, he called his family with exciting news. He was being transferred to Toledo, Ohio and would be able to live near family once again. He talked to everyone in the family on the phone that night and they were all expecting to celebrate Thanksgiving together when he arrived. The last call he placed was to his mom.

In Florida Phil, Jr. was preparing for bed, anticipating the long drive to Michigan the next day, when there was a banging on the door of the boarding house where he was staying. A man outside demanded Phil pay him money that was owed, before he left Florida. Phil protested that he had paid the money. When he returned with the receipt, the man pulled a gun and shot Phil, severing his spinal cord, killing him instantly.

Hearing shots, another man entered the room and witnessed the murder. The perpetrator turned the gun on the second man, but the gun jammed, and his life was saved. By this time there were a total of twelve witnesses who could later testify against the offender even though he fled the scene on his motorcycle. One of the witnesses picked up Phil's cell phone and noting the word "mom," returned the call to Annette and told her that her son was dead. Annette wouldn't believe him at first, but when he handed the phone to a policeman, Annette heard, "He died instantly, Ma'am. He never suffered any pain."

"It was really hard to forgive someone who would take a person's life like that," Annette says. "I found it was eating me up, so I asked God to forgive the man. It lifted it right off me. It was like the weight of the world was gone; I didn't have to carry that anymore. But it took me close to two years because it was a whole year before it went to court and it took me a year after that. My husband handled it so well. I was often envious about how he was on such an even keel after he re-dedicated his life to the Lord."

Phil had his own opinion about the punishment for the man who killed their son. "Just turn it over to God," he told Annette. "They have sentenced him to life in prison, but someone could forgive him and let him out, but we're not going to worry about it. We are going to leave it in God's hands if he should ever get out. The punishment is not up to us."

Annette still struggles with helping her son's children, young at the time of the murder, to cope with the absence of their father when they most needed him. She tells them, "Your dad wouldn't want you to be angry. Your dad's been gone for sixteen years now, and it's time for you to let it go. He is always with you, he's with me too, he was my first born, he's right here in my heart. I didn't want to see him die before his time. It wasn't his fault what happened. And he certainly didn't mean to have an argument with that guy that night. If you don't have anywhere you can talk to your dad, go over to the cemetery and talk to him there. Whatever you've got to do."

Annette took her own advice one evening following an especially tender moment in a Bible Study at her church. She couldn't stop crying. "It was about how the people didn't really appreciate the apostles who were following Jesus and they didn't trust Jesus." She asked herself, "Have I really forgiven? Is it really off of my chest, have I really given it all to God? Sometimes you backslide in your forgiveness, and I felt like I was getting angry and I didn't want to. I wanted to let it go. I thought I had to talk to my son." So, Annette went to the cemetery.

"I was doing a lot of praying besides crying. I was sitting with my car door open so I could see Phil's marker. I was originally thinking of kicking his tombstone but I had a second thought about that. I might break my toe or something," she laughs. "I was so angry that some of his children were so messed up over his death. They were so angry at their dad for dying. I felt like the anger was coming back on me and I didn't want it back. You'd think that because I'm in church this shouldn't be the devil's work, right? But I did feel the devil was trying to make me angry. I told Phil that night, 'If there's a way you could get to your boys, to let them know it's okay, and that you're always with them, I wish you'd do that."

"I was in the cemetery quite a while and the police came. I rolled up my windows and locked my doors because I didn't know who the headlights were from. A police officer came and tapped on my window. I rolled my window down and the officer said, "Pardon me Ma'am, but this is a dawn to dusk cemetery." Annette explained she didn't know that. He said," Are you alright?"

She said, "No, I can't quit crying and I can't go home until I quit crying. My husband will be really upset with me if I come home in tears." They offered to drive her home, but she did not want to alarm Phil. Eventually she went on home and they did follow her to make sure she was safe.

"When I got home my husband said, 'Well, it looks like you had a nice Bible Study, huh?'

I said, 'Yes, it was good.'

"Then he said, 'No, Annette, you have red eyes. It was more than good.'

"I said, 'Yes, it was a very touching study. I got a little emotional and I tried not to come home until I could not be emotional and as you see, I finally made it.' " And she laughed.

"He said kindly, 'Do you want me to pray for you?'

"I said, 'Yes, would you please?' "

After Annette's father's death in 1994, Phil and Annette moved to Onsted, Michigan to take care of Phil's mother who had dementia, and that is where Annette lives today. Phil died almost eight years ago and so Annette goes often to Monroe where all her family live, to enjoy family get-togethers. "We are a close family," she says. "That is how we got through the murder and the trial, calling each other every day and checking to make sure we are all okay" and they still do that today.

Her sons miss their dad, especially when they have a problem at work that requires a formula with which they know their dad could have helped them. Phil was also handy around the house. Annette relied on him to keep things in good running order, something she struggles with now that that responsibility is hers. The greatest loss, however, was his ability to remember Scriptures that would help people. Many people came to Annette after Phil's death and told her how he changed their lives. People will say, "We sure do miss Phil, and his prayers."

Annette smiles her sweet smile, her now grey hair touching her shoulders as she replies, "You are not alone, so do I and my kids." Annette continues to faithfully pray for her family, giving them wise advice even when it is not something they want to hear!

Annette gave each of her children one of their father's Bibles. The Bibles were well worn and filled with notes from Phil's daily readings over the years. One morning, son Bob was thumbing through his copy and in 2 Timothy 4:6-8 the entire passage was highlighted. Bob was dumbfounded. He called every member of the family to share the message. "Mom," he said, "I am positive that when you gave me the Bible nothing was highlighted. Do you suppose it is a message from Dad for us?" His siblings were delighted to hear the message. They got out their copies of their dad's Bible, to search for messages that had special meaning for Phil and might provide a word of counsel for them and their children.

The passage Bob found highlighted says: "For I am already being poured out like a drink offering, and the time has come for my departure. I have fought the good fight, I have finished the race, I have kept the faith. Now there is in store for me the crown of righteousness, which the Lord, the righteous Judge, will award to me on that day—and not only to me, but also to all who have longed for His appearing." Everyone who knew Phil would say this was true of his life, a model for *all* to follow.

6

The Truth Will Set You Free – Melanie Schultz*

It was a lovely day for playing in the yard. Melanie, four years old with her brother just two, came outside to play with the thirteen-year-old boy from across the street. Looking back, Melanie is puzzled her mother did not think it strange that a boy that age wanted to play with such young children, but her mother had grown up in this neighborhood and it never occurred to her that there might be a problem.

The birds were singing, flying from one old tree to another, but Melanie could not hear their songs. From infancy she had problems hearing, and regular doses of antibiotics and surgeries did little to help. She was leery of people and would cling to her mother when others were around. Although it was enjoyable to be outside with her brother and the neighbor, Melanie may have had a sense of foreboding but, because she was only four, she cannot remember.

She *does* remember the teenager saying they would pretend they were married and her brother was their child. In the yard there was a playhouse built between three narrow, tall trees about fifteen feet off the ground. The ladder was made from short boards nailed to two tree trunks. The boy insisted they climb up into the tree house. As Melanie looked to the top of the ladder, she didn't think she could make it; she was afraid of heights. When she hesitated, the neighbor promised to help and finally, she began the climb. Once inside the treehouse the ground looked so far away that Melanie was seized with fear. How would she ever be able to climb down without falling? Her fear only increased when the teenager cornered her in the small space of the house and began to touch her in intimate places, also instructing Melanie where he wished her to touch him.

Melanie did not understand what was happening but she was frightened. She felt dirty. She wanted down from the treehouse but there seemed no way for her to climb down. She was crying now, asking the older boy to let her go. Finally, afraid Melanie's mother might hear her, he led Melanie down the ladder and she ran away from him, into the house.

The next time he came to play, when Melanie saw his face in the window, she was terrified and ran and hid. When her mother saw her stricken face, she suspected Melanie was afraid of him. Holding her daughter in her arms, consoling her, Melanie's mother learned the whole story. Taking her tiny daughter's hand, they went to visit the neighbors. Melanie's mother asked her to tell the boy's parents what happened in the treehouse. The boy's parents refused to believe her. They said, "Surely she means our younger son who might have touched her in play without understanding what he was doing."

Melanie pointed to the older boy, saying his name. "No, it was him." The parents said they did not think she was telling the truth, which angered Melanie. Even when her mother told Melanie *she* believed her, she could not understand why the boy's parents did not. Melanie lived in that neighborhood for many years. She recalls how she hated facing the boy when she and her brother were outside raking leaves in the fall. "You are always there," she would think to herself, "and your parents don't believe me." His presence haunted her.

When Melanie was six, her mother hired a girl from the neighborhood to watch her children while she was finishing her teaching degree. The memory of the girl's mistreatment did not surface for many years. When it did, Melanie remembered being in a dark room and then in a bathroom where there was blood on her panties. She was crying hysterically, trying to figure out what had happened. She remembers telling her mother, and then the girl did not come back. Desperate for someone to babysit, her mother hired the girl's father. Melanie remembers how afraid the man was to have her complain about anything. Looking back, she realizes he knew his daughter had molested her and was afraid Melanie would bring it out into the open. Melanie wonders why her parents did not have a babysitter they trusted from church. Certainly, the father of the girl who had injured her was not a good choice. Meanwhile, Melanie's father, a quiet man, deferred to his wife to handle the disturbing things happening in his daughter's life.

There were signs that Melanie was becoming even more withdrawn. At school she loved being on the merry go round, but when the other children played games, she stood beside the teacher supervising the playground. She wanted to make friends, but her hearing problems set her apart. Her parents had her tonsils removed in kindergarten but that did not help. Between second and seventh grade she had ear surgery just about every year. "A surgeon put tubes in my ears more than once," she says. "I had to have skin from behind my ear taken to make a new ear drum and the internal bones of my ears were replaced with artificial ones."

The school speech and hearing therapist wanted to get Melanie hearing aids, but her doctor at a prestigious clinic got angry at the suggestion. He told the school officials, "She is *not* a candidate for a hearing aid. I want you to stop writing me letters and calling me about this. It's *not* going to work." Melanie was content when the elementary school ear specialist recommended that she be kept inside the classroom during the winter. She loved reading and studying.

In junior high school the health nurse fitted Melanie with earphones and a little black box that would pick up the teacher's voice. Melanie says, "It was an embarrassment to me; it put the focus on me and I was shy to begin with. I *hated* the thing. If someone dropped a pencil, the sound was magnified and I would jump. With the earphones it was hard for me to hear conversations around the room." After one year, Melanie refused to use it anymore. She felt even more isolated and alone in her world of muted sound.

Teachers and school counselors talked to her parents about the fact that Melanie did not reach out to people. She was easily teased and often came home crying. When her mother asked her what was wrong, she didn't know what to say; she just felt very sad and would cry about nothing at all. Her mother tried to help Melanie make friends. She invited cousins for sleepovers to give her playmates. However, Melanie did not seem comfortable with other children and she continued to cling to her mother. During all this time, no one outside the family was told about the abuse that had taken place.

Melanie's family were Christians, active in their church. Every time the doors of the church opened her family was in attendance. When Melanie was nine, the pastor mentioned that everyone should read their Bible every day. Although Melanie saw her father read his Bible in the morning and pray before going to work, her mother had been raised in a church which did not emphasize Bible study. Up to this point, neither parent encouraged Melanie to read the Bible. Now Melanie took the pastor's advice seriously and began a routine of reading the Bible every night before bed. She began reading in the first book of the Bible, in Genesis, and when she could not understand a difficult passage, she would ask her mother. Her brother began to read with her and soon her mother joined them. The stories in the Bible were like a breath of fresh air for Melanie.

About this time her brother went forward at church and asked to be baptized. This intrigued Melanie. She asked her mother, "Mom, what do I need to do to get saved?" Her mother was not sure what to tell her, but said, "When the hymn of invitation is given at the end of the service, you should go forward and talk to the pastor."

Melanie says, "I did what my mother told me to do. I remember so clearly the pale yellow dress I wore that day." Melanie began to understand the love Jesus had for her, that he died on the cross to take away her sins and make her clean. It would still be a long road for the healing Melanie needed, but she had begun to understand that she was special in God's eyes.

When Melanie was twelve, to get exercise and to pass time while waiting for their parents at church, she and her brother began a routine of running around the church building until the family was ready to go home. In all kinds of weather, the two of them would race each other. Melanie says, "My brother was best at running long distances but I prided myself that I was faster than he, because I was a sprinter. During Wednesday evening choir practice, we might run for over an hour. On revival nights we ran every night." On one such evening Melanie's brother was about fifty yards ahead. Shadows had begun to gather around the corners of the church building and Melanie was noticing the chill of the night air. As she approached the church shed towards an isolated corner of the property, out of the darkness she heard a voice calling softly, "Melanie, Melanie."

Melanie said, "I almost stopped, but a nudge deep within warned me. I recognized the voice of a teenage boy whose father had recently announced God was calling him to be a pastor. I made a mental note to avoid the boy."

Several months later Melanie and her brother had worn themselves out with running. When her brother left to play with some of the younger children, Melanie climbed into their parents' car to rest. Slowly the car door opened and the teenage boy she had avoided climbed into the seat beside her and grabbed her forcefully. Melanie struggled to get free, but he was fourteen and much stronger than she, and she was weary from running. He began to kiss her and pull at her clothes. She managed to get the door open and escape. He laughed at her and let her know he had allowed her to get away. He, too, got out of the car, still laughing at her. Melanie says, "I had never heard a laugh like that. It was not a normal laugh but *evil*." She quickly got back in the car and locked all the doors. "He continued to walk around the car, watching me, laughing his hateful laugh." Melanie was trembling.

He finally left and although she was terrified, Melanie ran inside the church to find her mother and tell her what had happened. Her mother found the mother of the boy and the three of them went outside to the car. When Melanie's mother told the other woman what her son had done, his mother said, "Melanie, I am going to tell you that this is never going to happen again."

Meanwhile, Melanie's mother told her daughter not to tell anyone what had happened because it would split the church. Melanie says, "So, it was a private thing; again, it was not talked about." Summer came and the boy and his brother left town to spend the vacation with friends. By the time he returned, it was time for school to start.

The first week of school a girl was taken into a field near the school, raped, and stabbed many times. By the time she was found, she was dead. Melanie says, "The boy from the church hung around the crime scene, and the police finally arrested him for the murder. He was apparently proud of what he had done." At Melanie's church they had a meeting and the pastor quietly told the congregation of his arrest. The members of the church were in shock. Their pastor asked the members to sign a paper requesting that the judge sentence him as a juvenile. He was fifteen years old and the church members had trouble believing he could have done something like this. As they drove home, her parents again told their daughter, "Now you know, Melanie, this is never to be talked about because it would split the church."

Her parents went on to say they would not sign the paper because they were convinced this boy knew what he was doing. No one commented when Melanie said, "That could have been me."

All during the time of the trial, Sunday after Sunday, the mother of the boy stood waiting after church to talk to Melanie, sometimes with her arms outstretched to hug her. Melanie avoided her. She knew the mother was hurting, but Melanie was hurting as well and couldn't tell anyone because she feared her emotions were ready to erupt. Eventually the boy's family stopped attending and the parents were divorced.

The pastor occasionally visited the teen. Twice he brought back letters which he read to the congregation during evening services. Interspersed throughout the letters were the words, "Ha! Ha!" The words didn't seem to fit with the rest of the letter, so Melanie felt certain they were directed towards her. She forced herself to remain glued to her seat. Looking back now, Melanie is sure those words were meant for the whole church, because he was only sentenced to remain in a juvenile facility until he was twenty-one years old. He had fooled them all.

Melanie silently dealt with her pain. She remembered hearing her name called that dark night and pictured what could've happened to her. "He would've dragged me from the shed to the railroad tracks and I would've had a similar fate to that of the girl who was stabbed," she thought. Melanie couldn't help but ask herself, "If I had told, would that girl have died?" Memories of earlier violations re-surfaced and she asked herself, "Could I have stopped it? Is there something wrong with me? Just when I start to think the world is a great place, I am attacked again. Why does this happen to me?"

Melanie pushed the memories down but inside she was tormented. Although she had never been raped, her experiences affected her just as deeply. She saw herself as ugly. She continued to isolate herself. In the bathroom at school, Melanie seemed to fade into the background as she watched the other girls touch up their makeup or check their hair. She was depressed and spent more and more time alone in her room listening to contemporary Christian music, which seemed to console her.

Meanwhile, in junior high school Melanie discovered she enjoyed learning other languages. She took Spanish and then added four years of German. While her hearing impairment limited her ability to understand the spoken word, she had an aptitude for translating the written word. When she considered a future career, she was sure it would include languages.

In her junior year of high school, she heard about a summer exchange program and with her mother's encouragement she applied and was accepted to go live with a family in Costa Rica. That summer changed Melanie's life. She thrived in this new environment. She made clear to the host family her very strong Christian faith. Although they were Catholic, they arranged for her to attend an evangelical church near-by. Melanie's courage in practicing regular times of prayer and faithful church attendance gave her a new-found confidence. She even sang in the church choir, and while the hymns were familiar ones to her, the fact that they were in Spanish helped her comprehension and pronunciation. Her ability in speaking the language grew. She remembers dreaming in Spanish and struggling to write English in her letters home.

"All the homes in San José, the capitol of Costa Rica, opened out into the street," she says. "I enjoyed the views outside the city where my family lived, but thought to myself, 'If I lived in this rich neighborhood, I couldn't ignore the poverty of the shacks in the city that are visible from our doorstep. I would want to help the poor.' "

Melanie loved the lifestyle and the culture. "Life was very laid back. There was no time you had to be somewhere and every afternoon people took a siesta for a couple of hours. It was easy to make friends, and I made many friends."

Delighted to return home with a better mastery of Spanish and several pen pals' addresses, Melanie faced the world with fresh excitement. While her parents expected her to choose a college near home, she chose to study foreign languages at a small Baptist college with the Smoky Mountains in the horizon. Melanie didn't know what work she would do with her Spanish major, but knew this was what she wanted to study. She was in the South, among Christian people, and her first week there she made more friends than she had ever met before. It seemed to her that everyone wanted to get to know her.

With anticipation she signed up for a Bible class, certain that since this was a Southern Baptist college, the professor would share her beliefs. She did not realize there was a divide in the denomination and her college was part of a liberal faction. The professor began the class by enlightening his students about the errors that occurred in Bible translation. He pointed out that if someone omitted a mark or made a misdirected punctuation error, the meaning of a passage was totally changed. Melanie told him angrily, "My God would have a perfect Word."

He replied to Melanie, "I'm not saying He can't preserve his Word. I'm saying He didn't." Melanie could not accept such a statement.

Now Melanie wrestled with what she should do. Should she quit school and go home? It was expensive to attend college and her parents were sacrificing to send her; she hated to tell them she was quitting. In addition, she had many supportive friends among the students. The choice was hers and she decided to stay. Nevertheless, the professor's teaching began to wear her down. Day after day as she attended her Bible class, her spirits sank lower and lower. Doubts began to crowd her mind. "He's a professor and who am I?" she thought to herself. She longed for someone to teach her from the conservative point of view.

If the Bible isn't God's perfect Word, then that makes God a liar. If the Bible isn't true, then there's no point to living the Christian life. But the Bible is true! It has to be! she thought. Melanie continued her morning Bible reading and prayer, but had to force herself to open the Bible when she needed answers. She read the Psalms and the book of Job.

Sinking into despair, Melanie replayed the past that she had tried to forget. *Why me?* she asked God every morning. *Why am I still alive? Why don't you just kill me?* Melanie began listening to a few songs labeled as Christian music, even though they put her in a depressed mood. As the darkness closed in around her, she felt strangely comforted.

One evening after consuming nothing all day, Melanie listened to the dark music over and over with the lights off. Then she opened a prescription bottle and stared at the pills. She couldn't bring herself to take them all, so she swallowed half in what she later realized was a cry for help. She put the other half under her pillow and told herself she'd take those if she woke up in middle of the night.

Then she set her radio alarm as usual. As she turned the knob past "Radio On" to "Radio Alarm," she heard just three words: "Help for suicidals." In disbelief, she stopped and listened. A soft, comforting man's voice was speaking. Later she discovered this was the Christian radio program called "Night Sounds." Melanie suddenly realized God planned that exact moment for her to hear those three words. She believed God did care for her and she knew she was going to be okay.

The next morning, she told her roommate what she had done. Her traumatic past, the secrets that haunted her from childhood, and the questions she had about her faith and herself were now brought into the open. A friend who was a religion major talked comfortingly to her. A campus counselor provided a safe place for Melanie to share about her traumatic past. She began to see a psychiatrist and a doctor. That day amid a flurry of responses, Melanie began her road to recovery from the place of depression where she had lived for many years. Every possible outlet to help her was explored. She remembers that by afternoon she returned to her room for a much-needed nap!

"Later, as I left the dorm for supper with friends, God overwhelmed me with His presence outside. On this February day, the sun was shining bright against a brilliant blue sky, the birds were singing, and suddenly I was so very thankful to be alive."

Melanie dug into her Bible and searched for answers. In Psalm 139: 1-6 (KJV) she read: "O Lord, thou hast searched me and known me. Thou knowest my downsitting and mine uprising, thou understandeth my thought afar off. Thou compassest my path and my lying down, and art acquainted with all my ways. For there is not a word in my tongue, but, lo, O Lord, thou knowest it altogether. Thou hast beset me behind and before, and laid thine hand upon me. Such knowledge is too wonderful for me; it is high, I cannot attain unto it."

Melanie couldn't believe she had never noticed these words before. God knew her thoughts, knew how many hairs were on her head, and knew every little detail about her.

She read Isaiah 6: 8b (KJV) where the Lord asked, "Whom shall I send, and who will go?" and Melanie answered with Isaiah's response. "Here *am* I; send me!"

Now Melanie felt she had a purpose for living. She determined God wanted her to study to be a missionary in a Spanish speaking country. Unsure of which seminary to attend, she listened as one of her roommates recommended a seminary where her brother was a student. At the end of the year Melanie transferred to that seminary and spent a year there, soaking up Bible teaching. As part of a school sponsored mission project, Melanie began working with children from a low-income neighborhood and found fulfillment in this as a calling. Working with the children brought her joy.

Meanwhile a specialist in hearing at the university previewed her auditory history and was appalled at how she had been treated and what she had suffered. He arranged for her to have ear transplants from a donor and urged Melanie to leave seminary so that she could spend a year focusing on the surgery and recovery. As she left the seminary campus that spring, she drove by the housing development where she had worked with the children. In her spirit she felt God telling her she did not have to go overseas to be a missionary. He could use her wherever she was. "My willingness was all He needed from me," she says.

The ear surgery was successful. Melanie laughs as she says, "I did not know birds sang all day long, not just in the morning."

Melanie began to see the lies that had kept her bound in silence. Her current pastor counseled her, telling her that her former church should have been told the truth about the boy who had cornered her in the car. While Melanie's mother thought revealing the truth would divide the church, the reverse was true. "Sin likes darkness," Melanie's pastor told her, "and so when the church was not informed, the secret allowed this young man to continue to harm others." Melanie realized the anger and frustration she felt was not toward the boy nor his mother, but against the church for not recognizing the boy's sin. Melanie had felt paralyzed because she was not allowed to tell the truth. In time Melanie was able to forgive the mother of the boy. Today, she wishes she could find the woman to tell her she is forgiven.

After her mother's death, Melanie took care of her father who lived in the same house where Melanie had grown up. Across the street still lived the family whose son had cornered her in the treehouse. When her father died, she took a Christian pamphlet over to the father of the family. "My father would want you to have this," Melanie told the neighbor. It was common knowledge this man had children from many different women, and this knowledge helped Melanie to forgive the son. She also wanted to show compassion to the father so that he would know she had forgiven him.

As Melanie forgave those who had injured her, God provided a husband who valued Melanie and who shared her dedication to seeking truth from Scripture. Melanie's husband has also helped her heal from her past.

Looking back at her painful history, Melanie has advice for anyone who has suffered abuse. "As a victim, you have to talk; you have to trust another person, you can't keep it hidden; it has to be shared. Psalm 139 is an important psalm to read, to see that you are special in the eyes of God. He knows everything about you including your feelings. I would encourage you to talk to someone, do not keep it a secret."

Furthermore, she says, "There is nothing wrong with you. A friend told me, 'The reason it happened to you is that you were innocent.' I believe that. The victim needs to know the reason why it happens, is that you are innocent."

Melanie also says, "Read the Bible. It is so important to see what God is saying to *you.* For me, it helps to get the truth out there. The more I talk, the more I learn I am not alone. There are many people, men and women, who are abused. Keeping the secret is what hurts us.

"To parents of abuse victims, make sure there is no guilt (put on the person abused). Make sure you let them know you believe them.

"Talking about it brings healing. If you are doubting your faith, pray and ask God to show you the truth. If you are suicidal, never, ever give up. You never know, the most amazing life is just ahead. Learn to find joy in everyday life. I find it, not just in the sunshiny days but even in the dark night skies or grey dismal days. With the Lord, I find the best days of life are just ahead."

John 8:32 (KJV) is a key verse for Melanie: "Ye shall know the truth and the truth shall make you free." As she sensed that God had a purpose for her life, Melanie was able to face the truth of what had happened to her. Supported by friends and healthcare professionals, she found the courage to put the past behind her, to see it for what it was, and to thank God she had survived. The truth that God knows her intimately and loves her just as she is, brought healing to Melanie. Now, she is thankful she can help others by sharing her story.

* Name has been changed.

7

Gems of Inspiration

Glory Be!

– Lucinda Pratt

Seems like when you reach some of the lowest points in your life, God has a way of lifting you up. On what felt like one of the saddest, gloomiest days in my life, I experienced just that.

The previous day had been the last Sunday for us to worship under the leadership of our church's beloved minister of over twenty-five years. His wife, with whom I taught, was retiring and they were planning to move closer to one of their daughters and the grandchildren. Our pastor was planning to continue his work there serving as an interim minister.

I sang in the choir and we had been asked to perform for both farewell services that Sunday. Our minister had even picked the music he wanted us to sing. It was his favorite song, and a special arrangement of "My Tribute" by Andraé Crouch had been purchased in memory of his father. The chorus declared, "To God be the glory, for the things He has done." The service was an emotional experience. A lot of tears were shed and having to sing and witness the departure ceremony for two services just compounded the grief. Many of us went home that Sunday with red-rimmed eyes and very stuffy noses.

The following day dawned very cloudy and dreary and there was a lingering sadness in the air. I had an appointment in a town about an hour away. With my stuffy nose and puffy eyes still in evidence, I wasn't looking forward to the drive. About halfway there I came over a hill and noticed a semi-truck in the lane to my right. The cab and the trailer were completely white except for some black letters down the side of the trailer and on the cab door. As I passed the big truck, I glanced up at the side of it and *I couldn't believe my eyes.* The bold letters said, "To God Be the Glory." The cab door repeated the message and when I looked up at the driver, he looked down on me and smiled. Even more miraculous, at that very moment the sun peeked out from behind the clouds and shone brightly on us until I'd passed by and rounded a curve in the road. As I continued on up the highway and the sun disappeared, the first thought that came into my head was the opening line from the song "Tomorrow" in the musical "Annie:" "The sun will come out tomorrow."*

I felt an instant renewal to my spirit. I believed God was assuring me that it's not the end of the world when you lose something. Things will get better and we owe it all to the Glory of God. He's always there for us and will always take care of us.

* "Tomorrow" – Lyrics by Martin Charnin and music by Charles Strouse

God with Me

– Marilyn Ann Troska

It was a lazy Saturday morning in May, 1996. As Marilyn Troska lingered in bed, resting for a short time, the thought came to do a BSE (Breast Self-Examination). "I knew this was something I should do on a regular basis," Marilyn says, "but I rarely did it." Life seemed hectic since she had begun working a 9:00 – 5:00 temporary office job five days a week. In addition to her job, there were many things to attend to at home, among them getting two daughters ready to leave for college.

"As I began the exam, I felt what seemed to be a rectangular lump on the outside of my left breast. I immediately knew that it was cancer." She called her General Practitioner for an appointment but after a breast exam, the doctor nonchalantly told her they would wait and see. She could go home, but she should monitor the area. He said, "Call me and let me know if there are any changes."

"I was afraid and needed God's help to get me through," Marilyn says. "I continued to drive twenty-five-minutes up and back to work every day, deciding most days to leave five minutes early. This allowed me to attend the 5:30 PM Mass at my home Church, St. John the Baptist in Costa Mesa, California. The extra weekday Masses kept me close to the Lord. I felt Him telling me that my breast lump *was* cancerous and that He'd be with me every step of the way."

Meanwhile, within a week or two of her first appointment Marilyn called her doctor to say there *were* changes in the lump, even though she could not detect any. Marilyn says vehemently, "This was the first bold-faced lie I had told in my entire life!" On the second appointment, when the doctor examined her, his eyes got big and he referred her immediately to a surgeon.

Marilyn made the appointment so she could go there on her way home from work. She thought she would just include it in her usual schedule in the most convenient way possible. When she confided her plans to Jacqueline, a close friend and prayer partner, Jacqueline asked Marilyn if her husband would be going with her to the appointment. If not, she offered to go with Marilyn. This alerted Marilyn to the fact that she might need extra moral support, and she asked her husband, Jim, to meet her at the surgeon's office. He, too, recognized the importance of what they would hear and readily agreed.

The surgeon had a lot of experience with breast cancer. Without needing the affirmation of the biopsy, he told her what she already knew: Marilyn had breast cancer. He asked her when she'd like to have the surgery, and Marilyn said as soon as possible. Since the surgery date was scheduled for the next week, he referred her to a plastic surgeon to see if that might be needed.

"The surgeon further stated that only a lumpectomy would be required but since my breasts are small, and clean margins are needed around the lump, the only real course of action would be to take the entire breast, a mastectomy. I agreed and also agreed to a tram flap reconstruction surgery using fat cells in my lower abdominal region to reconstruct a breast." Marilyn chose to have both operations at the same time, making the total time of the surgery about seven hours. As close as Marilyn and Jim are, Marilyn was conscious of how stressed her husband was with just one surgery. "I felt that he could not have emotionally gone through two separate surgeries for me; one was bad enough."

"I was very glad I had Jim with me, because the diagnosis was difficult to hear; I was shaken. Through the grace of God, I was able to drive the rest of the way home.

"After recovering from surgery for a month or so, I started chemotherapy twice a month for six months. Even here God was with me. The oncologist I was referred to came with accolades from many persons, including his patients. However, his waiting room was often so filled that it was standing room only, leading me to feel like it was a 'cattle call.' In addition to the chemo twice a month, I had a visit once a week with a shot to increase my white blood count. Later, I was able to start doing the shot at home myself to eliminate one visit to the oncologist. I started to feel sicker; I would lose my lunch about six hours after the chemo, and the anti-nausea drug was not helping.

"After three months, midway in my chemo treatments, my oncologist informed me that he 'could no longer deal with my insurance.' I had no idea what he was saying until he repeated it again. He was letting me go on a Friday before my next chemo treatment the following Wednesday." Marilyn walked out of the oncologist's office in shock. One of the women from the front office staff followed Marilyn, asking if she was okay. "I was so upset I could not give her a reply," Marilyn remembers. Even after a trip to the restroom to compose herself, Marilyn could not grasp that her doctor, on whom she depended to treat her cancer, had so dismissed her. "How could he give up on a patient just because of insurance?" she wondered.

She tried to quiet her nerves as she drove out of the parking lot, praying for help to make the drive home. Then, unbelievably, there close to the doctor's office was a Catholic church, beckoning her as a refuge. She had never noticed the church before but with a thankful sigh, she pulled into the parking lot, opened the heavy wooden doors, and entered the peaceful interior. As she knelt in the pew, she sensed the Lord gathering her under His wing of protection. Her rapid breathing slowed and she knew all of this would work out for the best. Confident that the Lord knew everything about her needs for treatment, she could now rest and trust Him to take care of her.

When she got home, she called Jim at work to tell him the news. He understood her dismay and said he would call his insurance representative immediately. The representative was dumbfounded at the news. She promised to have a new oncologist for Marilyn on Monday with an appointment on Wednesday for her fourth round of chemotherapy.

Later, Marilyn realized her oncologist was billing her insurance for too many unnecessary appointments, and her insurance was letting the doctor know, so he decided to drop her. "My new oncologist was wonderful. He put me on a new anti-nausea drug that really worked and he had me come in only twice a month for the necessary chemotherapy. I saw a light at the end of the tunnel—God's light guiding me to healing.

"I am now cancer free for twenty-four years. I could not have made this journey without God, my faith, the care of my wonderful husband, support of friends and the members of the weekly Breast Cancer Support Group at Fountain Valley Medical Center in Fountain Valley, California. This journey with the Lord reignited my faith and prayer life. Knowing that God is with me in and through everything and anything that life and the evil one might throw at me, I know God is still in charge. I'm no longer reticent to share what the Lord has done in my life. Praise God!"

A Whispered Prayer

– Marilyn Ann Troska

The seven-year-old child knelt at the altar. Her curly hair, falling just past her shoulders, was covered with a lace veil, her innocence emphasized by the folds of her white communion dress. As the sun streamed through the stained-glass windows, it painted the quietly attentive congregation in overlays of crimson red, deep green, and royal purple. From their niches decorated with ferns and lilies, graceful statutes of saints silently witnessed the centuries old sacred moment of children receiving their First Holy Communion.

Just moments before, Marilyn Goode had been in bed with a possible diagnosis of rheumatic fever. Her heart was in her throat as her Polish-American mom pleaded with the doctor to allow their daughter to take part in the ceremony she had so long anticipated. Once approval was given, promising she would obediently return to her bed once the last blessing was said, Marilyn had dressed and solemnly taken her place in the line of children filing up the center aisle of St. Raymond Roman Catholic Church in northeast Detroit.

Later, as from the exile of her bedroom Marilyn listened to her family celebrating downstairs, she clutched her rosary and prayed as tears formed in her eyes. For the first time in her young life, she truly felt the close presence of God.

In 1969 Marilyn married a young man from Pennsylvania whose career carried them all the way to California, and it was there that their two daughters, Heather and Carla, were born. On a Saturday a couple of weeks before Easter when the girls were four and six, Marilyn decided on impulse to go shopping. Although many Christians have the tradition of purchasing new clothes for Easter, Marilyn had not always followed that custom. Looking back, she doesn't know what made her decide to go shopping that Saturday, but she chose to buy one piece of clothing for each of them to mark the special spirit of the Resurrection. Marilyn's husband, Jim, was the scoutmaster of Boy Scout Troop, #515 in Santa Ana, California. The troop was camped out for the weekend and so Marilyn decided to do something special with her daughters and that motivated her to venture forth into the preholiday bustle.

Marilyn was conscious of time that Saturday morning as she chose the small J.C. Penney store in a mall near their home. Traffic congestion was a fact of life in this area of California, and she wanted to be home by 11:00 A.M., before the roads were clogged. As she jumped into the car, she thought to herself that she would normally have reached for a cigarette. The dangers of second-hand smoke were not widely accepted, and it never occurred to Marilyn that she was putting her two little girls at risk for lung cancer by always smoking in the car. She *did* know that smoking was affecting *her* health. Her doctor had warned her that her frequent bouts of bronchitis were a result of smoking a pack a day for the last twenty years. Marilyn truly wanted to stop but had recently given up trying, crying out to God, "*I can't do this.*"

That prayer was not even on her radar screen as she remembered she was out of cigarettes and would need to buy them in the midst of their rushed schedule. As Marilyn backed out of the driveway, she considered her alternatives. She knew she could quickly drive into the 7-11 convenience store just a few blocks away. She rejected that alternative. Reverting to the thrift of her Polish background, she did not want to pay the elevated price for a single pack, nor did she want to pay for a full carton at the convenience store. She shrugged off her discomfort and concentrated on the mission for the morning.

Usually taking the girls shopping was a test of Marilyn's patience. They loved playing hide 'n seek amidst circular racks of clothing. It took valuable time to corral them, not to mention the struggle to keep civil. But today was surprisingly different: her daughters seemed excited at the prospect of finding something to make Easter special, and Marilyn was pleasantly surprised at how quickly just the right article was found for each of them. The skirt Marilyn bought for herself would remain a silent reminder of this special day for many years to come. Driving home that Saturday morning, Marilyn passed the local 7-11 for the second time and once again rejected the idea of stopping to buy a pack of cigarettes.

Marilyn had the house to herself once they had eaten supper and the girls were down for an early evening bedtime. As she moved around the kitchen and family room, putting things in order, the cravings for a cigarette rose up again. She reasoned she couldn't very well leave her young daughters alone while she ran out to the store. She began to take inventory of the ash trays. Surely, she would be able to find at least one cigarette butt that would give her some relief. No luck! She and her husband always smoked right down to the filter.

Faithful Prayer Partners for many years (lt. to rt.): Jan Taylor, Reatha Meyer, and Marilyn Troska.

The next morning, Marilyn started to cough. She thought, "Here comes the bronchitis." She suffered through till Thursday when she had an appointment with their General Practitioner.

The doctor listened to her lungs and then said, "You know, it *would* help if you stopped smoking."

Marilyn said, "I did!" As those words came out of her mouth, she thought to herself, "Who said that? I was in disbelief!" The truth sank slowly into Marilyn's heart. She had not had a cigarette since Saturday.

She says, "My Lord heard my silent prayer and came to my aid even though I was not totally conscious of it. I remained smoke free for years, without cravings, even though my husband continued to smoke. It has been thirty-eight years since that day and I thank God that I'm no longer a smoker and no longer get bronchitis. I Praise God for the good health I enjoy.

The Blood of Jesus

The prayer meeting had left Mary Ann* feeling inspired and thankful to be serving the Lord. A small group of her friends were chatting when one of them said something that captured her attention. "I have been addicted to my fork," the friend said with a laugh, "and then someone gave me the prayer that breaks addictions. It goes like this: 'Blood of Jesus, cover me and give me the strength to overcome this temptation.' Then I just praise Jesus for setting me free. It works every time. The temptation to overeat is lifted off of me and I have the strength to resist eating any more than is good for me!"

Mary Ann looked at her friend thoughtfully. "*Surely, I don't have an addiction, or do I?*" When her husband had suggested they give up smoking, she knew it was a good idea. Everyone knew smoking was bad for your health and cigarettes were expensive. But it was much harder than she had thought. Lately, she was ashamed to admit she had been sneaking a cigarette when her husband was at work, letting him believe she was not smoking. Was she an addict? Deep within she felt the conviction of the Holy Spirit that, indeed, cigarettes had a hold on her that she couldn't break in her own strength.

Next day, when her husband left for work, Mary Ann's first thought was, "At last I can have a cigarette." Then she remembered she had vowed to ask the Lord's help to break this addiction. The temptation was strong to give in to her desire. Taking a deep breath, she prayed aloud, "Blood of Jesus, cover me and give me the strength to overcome this temptation to smoke. Thank You, Lord Jesus, for setting me free." And just like that, the temptation left her. She was thrilled. Throughout the day, she praised the Lord for her new freedom. Whenever the urge to smoke came, she repeated the prayer, and every time it worked.

Although the urge to smoke returned in the days ahead, it got weaker and less frequent. Several months later, she thought she was totally free when, standing next to someone smoking in a public place, the craving came back forcefully. In her spirit she heard "Think how much you enjoyed a cigarette." Undaunted, under her breath she said "Devil, you are a liar. I am free." Once again, she prayed the prayer for the strength to resist, and breathed a breath of relief when the urge left her. Yes, it had given her joy in the past, but a false joy. She was no longer a slave to cigarettes.

Today Mary Ann is totally free from the temptation to smoke, and when others confess they are struggling with a temptation, she shares the prayer that set her free. *"Blood of Jesus, cover me and give me the strength to overcome this temptation. Praise you, God, that I am free!"*

* Not her real name.

Messenger on a Harley

– Jan Edith Taylor

My friend had a special story to tell, a true story. I listened as she described a drive to an Adult Children of Alcoholics meeting on a late summer night in Michigan.

"The sun had begun to set. I peered carefully at the rows of trees that lined the property of St. Mary's Academy for Girls, looking for the narrow strip of asphalt that would allow me to drive into the grounds. Although hours of daylight lingered into the evening, shadows were beginning to make the unlighted entrance difficult to find. Finally, I saw it!

"As I carefully followed the one-way route to the back of the property, I felt as if I were on holy ground. The statuesque brick building that had once held an international boarding school for girls, rose majestically at the end of various avenues. Four stories of windows gazed solemnly at me as if I was a trespasser, their interior dark and empty. During week days the first two stories housed a private Catholic high school for female students. At the back were additional rooms where the Immaculate Heart of Mary (IHM) sisters held classes for immigrants wanting to learn English. Sometimes on weekends evening lamps could be seen on the third floor if there were churches occupying the building for weekend retreats. The majority of the rooms, with their thick walls, two-foot window sills, and cozy water-based heat, were unoccupied.

"The nuns were good stewards of the elegant structure. The main marble staircase was to be used only by senior students who had earned that right; the spotless parlors were furnished with elegant, upholstered furniture, ready for meetings and special events. Nevertheless, it was a financial challenge to maintain such a mammoth construction.

"The Adult Children of Alcoholics meeting would be held in the cafeteria, located at the back of the building. Several years before a 12-Step group had been started for those who had grown up with a parent or parents who were alcoholics. One of the IHM nuns had information on forming a group. She gathered a core band of interested people, and it took off from there.

"On this particular evening, I was returning after not having attended in many months. I worked full time, was raising two teenage children, and supporting my husband in his career which required travel and lots of time away from home. My days were full and somehow, I had neglected ACOA meetings, but that evening I was looking forward to being with the group.

"I pulled my car into one of the niches formed by the undulating tall brick walls. I was glad for the friendly welcoming light coming from the tall cafeteria windows that illuminated the dark, forest-rimmed road. It meant that my friend, the nun who led the meeting, had already arrived and was beginning the set-up for the meeting. I entered the cavernous room, my eyes searching out the corner where the table would be waiting for members to take their places. The sister, a middle-aged woman with short dark bobbed hair and a sweet smile, greeted me. We were the only two people in the room. I had arrived early so that I could help with arranging materials and chairs, and to have a chance to chat before the meeting began. As we fell into the pattern of preparing for the meeting, I asked the sister how things had been going with the group.

"She said the meetings were going well with a solid core of people attending each week, but she hesitated, 'I do need you to pray about this evening's meeting. There is a young man with some serious anger issues. The older man who calms him down is not able to be here tonight. Please pray that there will be no problems.' I began to pray silently in my spirit.

"By then people were beginning to drift in, some I knew and some that were new to me. The meeting had just started when there was the thundering interruption of a motorcycle's roaring engine, echoing off the brick fortress walls of the building. Everyone looked toward the door of the cafeteria with curiosity, and were quite taken aback by the commanding presence of the man who strode in. First of all, he was huge, standing well above six feet with a muscular chest, covered in a sleeveless leather vest. In his hands he humbly carried his motorcycle helmet and all eyes in the room were drawn to bare muscular arms that were tattooed from wrist to powerful biceps. He was African-American with a full afro and beard that completely surrounded his face. People tried not to gape, thinking, 'Is he in the right place?'

"Already I had identified the young man with the anger issue to whom the sister had referred. There was an empty chair beside him and the newest arrival, with a nod to the group and a quiet apology for coming late, slipped into that seat. As the meeting proceeded, thoughts and experiences were shared and everyone watched uncomfortably as the young man would take issue with something that was said. He would make heated comments reflecting hurts from his past. His imposing seatmate would then speak quietly to him, and the problem was instantly diffused. This went on throughout the meeting, and the ACOA members began to relax. The result was a good sharing of experiences and the hour passed quickly. When the time came to dismiss, everyone got up, slid their chairs in, and talking companionably made their way to their cars outside the doors of the cafeteria. The impressive visitor was one of the first people to leave. I drove home thinking in awe, what did I just witness?

"A couple of weeks passed and again I decided to attend the ACOA meeting. I was drawn partly by my curiosity to find out more about the man on the motorcycle. Again, I arrived early to help the leader with the set-up, giving me the perfect opportunity to ask about the motorcyclist who had come that night. I asked the sister, 'Is this someone who normally comes to meetings?'

"She looked at me with a twinkle and a smile, and said, 'No, he's never been here before that night, and he's never returned.' She paused and then looked me squarely in the eye, 'I think he was an angel.'

"As unusual as his whole appearance was to my usual concept of an angel, something in my heart told me the sister was right. In answer to our prayers and the situation in the ACOA group, we had been visited that night by a heavenly presence, on a Harley Davidson!"

For more information on the twelve-step program for Adult Children of Alcoholics and to find a meeting near you, visit their website: https://adultchildren.org.

8

An Answer to Prayer – Derek Greene*

The elderly man awoke shaking, every nerve on alert. *He knew that Voice*! It was the voice of God speaking to his spirit: "Pray for Derek *right now*!" The Pentecostal minister obeyed instantly. Brushing graying hair back from his eyes, he fell to his knees on the shag carpet in the parsonage bedroom. He paid no attention to the clock on the pine nightstand that read 1:00 am, nor to the mid-winter chill of the bedroom. He ignored his wife's sleepy questions arising from the darkness on the other side of the bed. He concentrated on drawing close to God, praying in the Spirit, knowing the Spirit would know what intervention was needed for his grandson, Derek Greene.

Derek's grandfather sensed it was a matter of life and death. Although he shook with a nervous chill and could almost see the dark presence of fear stalking nearby, he chose to focus on the God of miracles and disciplined himself to the task of intercession. God had awakened him so that he could pray for his twenty-one-year-old grandson. He might not know where his beloved Derek was or what threatened him but he was confident God knew and his prayers would be heard.

On that same night of January 24th, 1988 Derek was at a strip club near the naval base in Portsmouth, Virginia, where he served as a medical corpsman. The opening and closing of the door to the club brought in the fresh chill of an ocean breeze, soon corrupted by the odor of cigarette smoke and heavy perfume. From the bar Derek looked around at the crowded tables, enjoying the view of beautiful women moving on stage as well from table to table. He was amazed at how at ease he was. As a teenager he was uncomfortable around girls, but since joining the navy, he felt confident. He had grown three and a half inches and, while still shorter than many of his buddies, his daily regimen of weight-lifting and running had resulted in a firm and powerful body. The red-haired sailor also discovered that women responded to the respectful kindness he had learned from his southern, Christian up-bringing.

Derek's job at the hospital meant that he had to be constantly on high alert. The medical corpsman felt keenly the responsibility of giving his best care to the patients but here at the strip club, he could feel his body and mind relax, and he could breathe. There was a part of him that recognized the rage just below the surface from many painful memories: bullying at school because of his small size, abandonment by his father, and the many times in his life when the adults that should have protected him left him open to violence and abuse. Now the sweet aroma of marijuana mixed with the sour smell of beer and liquor permeated not only his clothes but his soul. Derek felt confident and relaxed, and knew this was the place he wanted to be, where he felt at home—the deception that when he was numb, he was in control.

Amidst the crescendo of loud voices, the pressure of crowded bodies, tables crunched together, and the haze of smoke, Derek was given a message that a friend had called from the projects in Norfolk, needing a ride back to the base. Derek knew better than to get behind the wheel of a car when he had been drinking, so he grabbed a friend and persuaded him to drive. Derek could sense his friend's fear. Both men knew the streets where they were going were the territory of violent gangs, but Derek felt invincible. He had already been in some violent fights and his temper had gained him the reputation of being a bad dude. The word was, *don't mess with him!*

Confident he could handle any problem that might come their way, he and his companion drove into the Projects. It was after midnight and in the darkness the two sailors were uneasy as they watched people moving around on the street: a person here and there clothed in a dark winter jacket, a knitted cap pulled around the face. At a stop light a sharp-looking Trans Am pulled up behind their car. Derek was convinced the car bumped them, the driver asking for trouble. His emotions on edge, his control impaired by alcohol, Derek was enraged. He jumped out of the car, his breath in the cold night air creating a fog around his head. He ran to the open window, waving his arms and shouting in a menacing manner at the other driver, *"What's the matter with you? I'm going to drag you out of that car."*

In response the driver pulled a gun and aimed it at Derek. Instinctively, Derek turned sideways to minimize the impact and when the gun went off, the bullet hit Derek in the side of the chest. The driver, looking shocked, dropped the gun on the seat of the car, and sped off. It was 1:00 in the morning, the same moment that in Kentucky Derek's grandfather was on his knees, earnestly praying for his grandson's life.

Everything slowed down for Derek. A calm settled over him. He wrote down the make of the car and the license number, and then holding onto the roof of the car to keep himself upright, Derek climbed into the passenger seat. His voice firm, avoiding the panic that threatened to rise up into his throat, Derek told his friend, "I've been shot. Listen to my instructions or I'm going to die."

Although the driver was also a corpsman, he began to panic. Blood was coming out of Derek's mouth signaling a punctured lung. Derek also noticed that the bullet had passed through his chest and had come out on the other side. He knew he was in serious trouble and time was of an essence. When he saw a police car drive into a nearby 7-11, with relief he knew this was the help he needed.

He told the officer, "I've been shot in the chest. I have a sucking chest wound. You will need to cover both the entrance and the exit wounds. Now, I am going to lie down and get my feet above my head to prevent shock. *Do you understand me?*" The policeman called an ambulance and Derek was taken to Portsmouth Naval Hospital. A chest tube was inserted and the young man was stabilized.

Derek had not wanted his mother to know what happened, but after three days, the hospital notified her. That is when Derek learned that at the exact time of the shooting, his grandfather had been praying for him.

The tie between Derek and his grandparents went back to his earliest childhood. Derek's father returned from Vietnam with what today is called Post Traumatic Shock Disorder (PTSD). Derek says, "My mother was a Midwestern girl who had no concept of war. Now that her husband was home again, she expected him to settle down, get a job, care for his family, and get on with his life. And he wasn't able to do that."

After Derek's birth in 1968 his father suddenly disappeared. He escaped from his responsibilities as a new father to reunite with his army buddies on the military base at Fort Hood, people with whom he felt comfortable. Abandoned by her husband, Derek's mother moved to Mount Vernon, Indiana to live near her parents and to have help with her new born child. This became a pattern: his mother following her parents in frequent moves to various churches in which his grandparents served as pastors.

When Derek's father returned to the family a month later, they had moved to Lake Charles, Louisiana. Fortunately, the veteran was able to get a job as a drawbridge operator. The tranquil presence of the waterways soothed the former soldier. There was also no stress in his job as he responded to the passage of the boats. "This was the right job for him." Derek says. When Derek's grandparents decided to move back to Indiana, his dad tried to persuade his wife to remain in Louisiana but in the end, they moved with her parents.

In Indiana the problems in the marriage began to escalate. Derek was in second grade riding his bike back from school when he saw his father driving by with a strange woman in the car. He innocently told his mother what he had seen. Derek's mother followed her husband and discovered he was having an affair. The couple separated and Derek's mother was devastated. Derek was sent to live with his grandparents.

Derek's grandmother was a strict disciplinarian. You could not take anything out of the refrigerator until she gave permission, and when Derek threatened her control of the household, she beat him with a broom and any other implement that was handy. Nevertheless, after experiencing the lack of stability in his own home and his father's indifference, Derek remembers being happy as a child, living with his grandparents. He was especially close to his grandfather.

The churches his grandparents pastored were Pentecostal but there was no denominational connection. Derek says, "Miracles were happening: people getting up out of wheel chairs, the blind seeing. But there was also a lot of legalism in the church. An emphasis on modesty dictated that men not wear short-sleeved shirts, and women could not wear jewelry. I was not allowed to play sports.

"As a result of the many rules," Derek says with a chuckle, "I'm probably the biggest hater of Christian *religion*! If the devil can't keep you from the knowledge of God, he will push you too far into developing doctrine that puts God in a box, that doesn't allow Him to be supernatural. The doctrines of the Bible are pretty simple, but much like with the Pharisees, people add a lot, to make sure they get it correct. My battle, my journey concerns a lot of conflict with *Christian religion*. While I was growing up, I saw mighty moves of God but at the same time I saw the heavy hand of legalism. I always had this tug or pull against God because the God that I knew was filtered through the paradigm of the church."

Meanwhile, at twenty-one Derek's rebellion continued. His near-death experience and his grandfather's prayers did not motivate him to change his lifestyle. He continued to party and hang out at bars and strip clubs. Later on, he would admit that he was thankful God was thinking about him on that night in January, protecting him in the midst of an evil that threatened to destroy him. The day would come when Derek was also able to understand that, in spite of everything, God was working to fulfill His purpose for Derek's life.

As a consequence of his actions in the Projects, the man who shot Derek was caught, tried, and found guilty. This man was also in the navy, moonlighting at another job in that dangerous neighborhood in order to provide for his wife and little daughter. Derek acknowledges that he, himself, created the situation by approaching the man's car in a menacing matter. In turn, the navy man meant to just threaten Derek, but the gun had a hair trigger, and it went off. The shooter received a bad conduct discharge from the military. He was given five years in prison which was probated, provided he did not get into any trouble over the next five years.

In tears Derek recalls watching his attacker with his daughter. "This beautiful little child looked like Shirley Temple. I saw her peering up at her dad and hugging him, and I knew he was a doting father. To this day I have to live with the fact that I tore up this family's life. It's awfully hard to get jobs when you've been charged with first degree assault. I know God has forgiven me, but I struggle with forgiving myself. Even when I was *not* walking with God I prayed, 'God, make it turn out okay for him.' "

Derek says, "Only by the grace of God did I make it out of the military without getting kicked out—without totally blowing up."

After eight years in the military, in 1993 Derek moved back to the Lexington, Kentucky area, to be near family. "I was totally into the bar scene. I became a bouncer, bartender, and just hung out. Every day that the bars were open, I was there, constantly partying, doing every kind of drug that is out there. I still worked out and ran to keep in shape.

"My mother made the mistake of putting me on her bank account, and I was using it to write checks. I was working construction, and I was good at it, making lots of money, winning money playing pool at a semi-professional level, and selling drugs to support my habits. I wanted to be the man who always had the stuff to give out at parties. Thousands and thousands of dollars were passing through my hands."

But the life he was leading took a toll. He finally reached a point where he was trashed out, done with the party scene, and he had blown all his money. He was living with his mom in Wilmore, Kentucky in a house she had built there. Wilmore is the site of Asbury college and seminary, and the community is a place where it is not unusual to see Scripture printed on the sides of buildings or on billboards. Derek's mom had returned to the church and was praying for Derek to do the same.

On July 4th, 1993 Derek decided not to go to work. He met a friend at a bar, and then they went into Lexington to a strip club. Derek knew some of the strippers. One in whom he was particularly interested, invited them to a party that would take place after the women got off work. The house in which the party was being held was palatial. The hostess' parents were politically prominent, absent from home while celebrating the Fourth of July holiday in Florida. They were unaware their daughter was hosting a party in their affluent suburban neighborhood. Derek and his friend arrived, looked over the crowd, got themselves a drink, and began to move around the comfortably furnished rooms. On one of the sofas Derek spotted the young woman in whom he was interested, but she was accompanied by a date. Derek watched the two of them for a moment. Her escort was young, a fifth of vodka by his side that was mostly gone. Derek says, "Vodka is a liquor that I avoided because it altered people's personalities for the worst. I thought to myself, 'there are other fish in the sea,' and I began to move on."

Derek's friend did not sense the danger and ended up on the same sofa next to the couple. It wasn't long before the young woman's inebriated date got into an argument with him. Derek moved closer to help his friend disengage. Derek says. "I had a buzz but I was not drunk, so I tried to back off from arguing with this guy. I told him we didn't want any trouble." As the young man walked away, laughing to other people about how he had bested Derek, something snapped in Derek. Following him around the corner, Derek said, "You just thought you knew what was happening inside of me,"

Emotions from childhood rose up to fuel Derek's anger. Derek grabbed the young man and with great force threw him down the stairs of the split level. Derek says, "I weighed about 172 pounds and the day before I had benched 265 pounds. I could run miles and miles – not a great distance, because I had short legs – but I had great endurance."

Derek described what happened next: "The house had a front porch and from the porch the yard went down steeply to the street and the guy was lying near the street. His girlfriend had climbed into the car and said to him, 'Come on, let's go!'

"When you get into a fight with someone, you never know what is inside that other person. While my friends restrained me, this guy pulled out a knife, but I didn't see it. I ran down to the street, grabbed the guy, and started hitting him in the face over and over. I felt him grab me and I thought he was trying to keep me from hitting him. It was like everything was dark except for the light around his face." But the man wasn't grabbing onto Derek, he was stabbing him over and over – fourteen times. He opened the flesh around Derek's femur so deeply that later Derek reached inside with his knuckles to stem the blood flow. The attacker drew the knife across Derek's back giving him a gashing wound that left an ugly scar. He stabbed Derek in his right shoulder, giving him a serious wound there. Many of the stab wounds were to Derek's left side where his lung had previously been punctured. Now the lung was punctured again as well as wounds to many of his other organs.

Derek's friends called an ambulance. "The ambulance rushed me to the University of Kentucky Hospital, to the trauma center. I was losing so much blood that the gurney sheets were soaked and people were making tracks in my blood as they walked in and out of the hospital.

"Because of my work in emergency in the navy, I knew when doctors asked for families to be there as soon as possible, it's not good and they are not liking the odds. My Mom and my sister were notified and they rushed to the hospital. When they came into the room, I felt a sense of dread, *and I knew I was going to die, and I knew where I was going.* I had rejected God in my life, and He *knew* I was rejecting Him. Your theology can be whatever it is, but I don't believe in deathbed confessions. The Bible says to *repent* (be willing to change). It doesn't say to simply confess and I had been powerless to change. My sister has a trained voice. She had sung opera and gospel songs. I asked my sister to sing for me; I figured this would be the last time I would ever hear her sing.

"They started pushing me down the hall to the Operating Room, and I remember, like in the movies, watching the lights go over my head.

The anesthetist started getting things ready, and as he held the mask for the gas, he said, 'Well, are you ready?'

"I knew what he was asking, but I did not expect to ever wake up, and I said, '*No, I'm not ready.*' I knew where I was going. I didn't even feel like I had the right to ask God (for forgiveness). I was just going to accept what was coming, 'cause I had lived this life.

"Then later, I have this fuzzy memory of people being beside me in this critical care unit (CCU) and being very swollen. I was foggy in my brain but I was aware, '*I'm alive*!'

"There was a man in my grandfather's church, who was a minister and an assistant to my grandfather. I had met him briefly one time. I was in surgery for nine hours and the whole time I was in surgery he spent praying in the chapel. That guy did not know me. Believe what you want, but I believe that man changed some things in the Spirit. I didn't know about this for a long time afterwards. He didn't come and tell me. I don't even remember how it was brought to me.

"I believe that that sense of dread I felt in the hospital was the death angel walking into that place. It's hard to explain, but I *knew* I was going to die that day, and something changed the course. As strange as it may seem, I did not hit my knees and turn to God.

"Now this one *did* scare me. I knew I could die, that my life was tenuous at best. We're such fragile creatures, and we can believe we are so invincible, but we are literally a second away from a freak accident or anything, to die and enter eternity. So, I'm living with this but I don't turn to God. I'm not going to turn to God out of fire insurance, just because I'm scared of going to hell."

Derek spent a long time recovering from his wounds, living in his mother's house. When he went back to work, he worked for the federal Department of Housing and Urban Development, traveling to paint buildings in various housing projects. "I'm still hitting the bars all over the place because it's all I know. It's who I've become; it's the life I've built. So, even when I am in a town where I don't know anybody, it's go out to the bars with the guys I'm traveling with; it's chase the girls. Food is paid for; places to sleep are paid for; and I'm blowing everything I've got. Finally, I'm just burnt out. It's the same thing over and over again. I've done everything."

On July the 12th, 1995 Derek was sitting on the back porch at his mother's house smoking a joint. "My thoughts were dark; I can't say I was suicidal but my thoughts were starting to go in that direction. I have to say—if you believe, if you take your own life it's only going to get worse, it does help. But I just wanted everything to stop! I didn't want to think nomore. I just wanted to go to sleep and not wake up for a long time.

"I had previously played around with some stuff I shouldn't have played with, that had to do with meditation, some martial arts, eastern mysticism stuff. I was getting into some wacko stuff. God had become a shaky concept to me. I still had just enough of a Christian basis that I would think, 'Am I opening the door to some things to visit me that I really don't want visiting me?'

"I was thinking about all this and I remember going, 'God, if you're real, I'll do anything you want me to do. But you can't be my grandpa's religion. You can't be my mom's experience. I gotta know that you are real, and not just some philosophical thing like eastern mysticism, Dahlai Lama, the Hindus. There's gotta be something solid here.'

"I don't know how to explain it to anybody else. And you can say it was the marijuana, or whatever you want, but the Creator of this Universe showed up. And there is not anything physically I have felt in my life that is more real than at that moment, the absolute manifest presence of God Almighty. The 'I AM' showed up.

"I understood that concept in Scripture when Moses stood before the burning bush and askes God, '...what shall I tell them (is your name)?' (Exodus 3:13)

"And we translate it as 'I AM. The Self Existent One, that, Beside-Me-There-Is -No-Other, I-Counsel–With-No-One.' (Information from Exodus 3:14)

"I knew it! The same way I knew that I was going to die that night in the hospital. And a conversation began that lasted for about twenty minutes. Not an audible voice, and I've never had God speak to me that way again. I've had Him lead me; I've had things that I knew, things spoken to me; I've had downloads of information that I knew were from God. But in that moment, there was something unique—the closest thing to explaining it is, that it was like telepathy. It was a conversation that was happening without restraint of physical time and space.

"Being the curious sort that I am, I said, 'Okay, God, there are 35,000 different variations of Christian denominations in the world. There are some major basics and then they are all split up into their little individual views of things. Who's right?'

"And all I got was, '***That Book is right.***'

" 'Really? That's all you're going to give me.' I didn't understand that was an invitation to seek God and to know Him for myself.

Because I wanted to know, 'God give me the right way and I'm going to do it! You give me the rules and I'll live it!' But He isn't about rules; He is about relationship. In Scripture He says, 'I'll write 'em (laws) on their hearts.' (Hebrews 8:10b) It will have to be a relationship. I didn't get that concept even then. I was sitting here talking to the Absolute Creator of the universe, but my paradigms were still stuff that had to be put aside and shifted and re-done.

"I had not walked into a church in I don't know how long. My mom wouldn't even hardly talk to me about it anymore because I was like, 'when I want it, I know where it's at, and I'll be there, and if I don't, you can talk until you're blue in the face and I don't give a crap.' My mom came in from church – it's Wednesday night - and I said, 'Well, Mom, I'll be going to church with you Sunday.'

"She goes, 'Okay.' And that was that. She told me later that she went in to her bedroom and started crying.

"*So, it's over.* I went to church."

While Derek wanted his life to change, his new Christian life was full of ups and downs. He married a Christian girl but there were so many differences between them that the marriage did not last. After the divorce, Derek started going back to the bars. He was getting arrested for driving under the influence and serving time in jail. One night in a bar he met his current wife, Jackie.

"After my first marriage broke up, I didn't tell anyone about God, or anything that I had previously done in the church. Jackie was recently divorced, and she's just going out with friends to commiserate, drinking a bit, maybe getting drunk now and then. But that wasn't her lifestyle and she was warned about me. So, we're together for two years, and we're living in Wilmore, Kentucky. One night, God showed up. I was at the bar, drunk, and all of a sudden I started quoting Scriptures and making statements about God, and my friends were flabbergasted." Derek started to talk about how important it is for lost people to understand that there's hell fire and damnation to be examined, and that churches have gotten a little loose on the love side. "This is all starting to come out while I'm intoxicated. The result is that there is this dam and a crack has occurred."

Meanwhile, Jackie heard all this and she was intrigued. Her background was Baptist, but she had heard Derek's sister and her husband talk about miraculous healings in their church, and she is curious about that. So, one Saturday she said to Derek, "Why don't we go to church?"

Derek was taken aback: "Good. We'll go to church." Derek thought, "She's probably going to choose one of the churches where she feels comfortable. They're out about noon and you can make reservations at the local restaurant and be there on time and not have to worry about the preacher going overtime."

Then Jackie surprised Derek, "Let's go where your sister and brother-in-law go."

And Derek thought, "Oh crap!

"Now the church that my sister and brother-in-law go to is *not* like the Pentecostal version that I grew up with," Derek says. From conversations with his sister, Derek sensed that God was truly present in the services and this made him afraid. But he loved Jackie, so he decided to go along with what she wanted.

Derek thought "This is going to scare the heebie-jeebies out of her. She's a good Baptist girl. This Pentecostal service could run two or three hours, with all the extra diversions. *We won't have to worry about this ever again.*"

"We get there, go in, and *the sweet loving presence of God* comes into the place but it's different. I had felt the power of God; I had talked to the Creator, Himself. *There was something different*—a love, a pulling, an acceptance, I don't know how to describe it. And I remember thinking to myself, *'I could do this.'*

"I look over at Jackie to see her reaction. People are raising their hands, the praise going on, a spattering of speaking in tongues during the worship. She was taking it all in, not getting involved, just looking around."

After the church service was over, Derek's sister, Theresa, asked Jackie, "How did you like it?"

"It was fine," Jackie said.

"Well, we're going to see this guy tonight. His name is Todd White," Theresa said.

Derek's family had previously described Todd White as having dread locks and that did not fit Derek's image of what a preacher in the pulpit should look like. "I thought my family were fruit loops for going to hear this guy. So, I was amazed when Jackie said, 'Yes, I wanna go.' I knew I would go if Jackie did but *I was not excited*.

"We got to the church that night and it was deader than 3:00. There ain't nothing moving. Yes, they're raising their hands, yes, they're clapping, but the Spirit of God just ain't there. I'm looking down the row at my sister, thinking 'What in the world you have drug me to? Now I have to sit through this; I have to miss the NBA playoffs.'

"Suddenly the Spirit of God walked into that place and I turned and I saw this little short dude with dreadlocks, and he was dressed like someone from the Bahamas. And I went, 'Him, God?'

Within my spirit I heard the answer. 'Yes.' "

Todd White got up to speak and Derek said, "Within five minutes I didn't even see him anymore. He exuded the love of God so powerfully, I thought this must be what Jesus was like when He was walking on this Earth: talking with the crowd, moving with compassion, and all of that. Right there started the change in me that there was this love of God, this compassion, that I had not grasped before. That night changed something because I saw Jesus in another human being in a way I had never seen Him before. I had seen God do miracles through other people, but I had never seen this love toward other human beings. As the saying goes, 'When the student is ready, the teacher will appear.'

"After that I began seeking God and this love." Derek began to pray, "I want *Your* heart toward other people, God; I really don't have it." Derek had always been very guarded, with walls of protection around himself. Now he began to see God as his defender. He started his mantra from before, "I've tried to do everything I can to live for you, God."

God spoke to his heart, "You're right, *you* tried but you never made Me your defender, your everything. You never gave Me all of your fears, your walls, your self-protection devices."

"From that point a journey began to change my very soul. In your spirit you're saved and you come into communion with God, but this taking on the mind of Christ, and Him changing and making you whole was something new. Now it was not trying to avoid hell and the Lake of Fire but literally changing you back into the creation that God intended from Adam."

Derek says, "God puts people in our lives to help us. People just show up in my life; God brings them to me." These are people who are doing drugs, alcoholics, people with emotional problems. "They know that I love them, and that God does not reject them, so neither do I, but I speak the truth to them. If they show up high to church, they may be able to fool some people but they can't fool me. I have been there and I'm willing to help, but they have to be honest with me and with themselves. Otherwise it is a waste of time. Jesus must be *Lord* of their lives. I don't fall for what I call 'Jesus talk'; that is just crap. When people are willing to be accountable, I am there for them. I'm not discarding them because they goof off."

Derek cites Romans 8:28: "And we know that in all things God works for the good of those who love him, who have been called according to his purpose."

"I was called for a purpose. All the things in my life have built and shaped me in two ways: first of all, they shaped me wrongly (In the Bible David said I was born in iniquity from my mother's womb – Psalm 51:5.). The security devices that we build are because of outside influences that press on us and cause fear." But secondly, Derek sees that God has used his experiences to make him more understanding of people's problems and short-comings. "I want others to be as free as I am, to be released from what has shaped them to be afraid, to build defenses."

It has been a long, hard road, but Derek has found peace and a living faith, following Jesus. Looking back Derek sees how God was with him throughout all the dark years, guiding and protecting him. And now he wants to be there to help others, just as his grandfather would have wanted.

9

Resurrection Hope – Jan Edith Taylor

I Corinthians 15:12 – 14 "But if it is preached that Christ has been raised from the dead, how can some of you say that there is no resurrection of the dead? If there is no resurrection of the dead, then not even Christ has been raised. And if Christ has not been raised, our preaching is useless and so is your faith."

The chimes rang out with the song, "What a Friend We Have in Jesus!" I stopped my unpacking in my dorm room, taking a moment to feel the wonder of it all. My mother loved this Christian college and she had wanted me to study here ever since I could remember. And here I was enrolled as a freshman, a dream finally realized.

The year was 1959 when many mainline churches were at the forefront of liberal arts education, complete, in this case, with two days of mandatory chapel services. I looked forward to it all.

The year before I had spent my high school senior year as an exchange student, living with two German Methodist families: one a pastor's family and the other a devout widow with two sons in their twenties. Their church took me in and treated me like a daughter; such love for a stranger totally overwhelmed me. One night I knelt in the pastor's cellar and said, "God, whatever this love is, I want more of it." God answered that prayer by drawing me closer to Him through His Holy Spirit and making the Bible come alive. I arrived the next fall on the Christian college campus eager to embrace everything a Christian education had to teach me. What I did not expect was the liberal theology that permeated many of the faculty's viewpoints.

A required course, "Religion in Modern Life," cast doubt on whether the miracles of Jesus' ministry were true. The professor said, about the resurrection, "We will find out whether it is true when we die." It was apparent he had his doubts. As for the virgin birth, he said that a number of heathen religions had a similar fable, and early Christians wove those myths into their newly embraced faith.

I continued to sense the Holy Spirit working in my life, sought out Christian friends among the upper classmen, and faithfully attended the college church. But in my proud desire to fit in with the intellectual atmosphere of college life, I began to be double-minded: while I spoke confidently of my belief in the power of prayer and considered myself a strong Christian, I began to doubt the basic tenets of the Christian faith. By the time I graduated I could spout liberal theology with the best of them.

In the book of James 1: 5-8 the Bible says, "If any of you lacks wisdom, he should ask God, who gives generously to all without finding fault, and it will be given to him. But when he asks, he must believe and not doubt, because he who doubts is like a wave of the sea blown and tossed by the wind. That man should not think he will receive anything from the Lord; he is a double-minded man, unstable in all he does." And I was unstable.

My husband, Ed, and I joined the Peace Corps following our graduation from college. After nearly five years of living in South America, we returned to the United Stated as the Vietnam War was winding down. Looking back, I suspect that part of my depression was culture shock, seeing my country rocked by division and strife over the war. However, even more disturbing was my lack of purpose. I continued to doubt God's love for me and did not recognize that, as a follower of Christ, my life was not my own. In my pride I was determined to be in charge of my own life, and that desire led me down many blind alleys. I participated in consciousness-raising sessions in the women's movement and spent many hours dedicated to political causes. My two pre-school children were allowed to express themselves without the consistent rules that would have given them and me the sanity and stability we needed. My husband traveled frequently with his job, and so I was often like a single parent struggling with the demanding job of raising two young children, in a new community where I did not know many people. In addition to all this, robbed of my faith in an afterlife, I was feeling hopeless. I remember thinking, "If this is all there is, were it not for my husband and my children, I could take my own life.

Because of my early training in the Christian faith, I sought answers by joining a church. The members of an adult Sunday school class became the target for my many questions. I often thought, "I have gone to church all my life. *There has to be something more.*"

One Sunday a gentle visitor to the Sunday School class read the well-known Scripture in Matthew 7: 7 & 8: "Ask, and it shall be given to you; seek and you will find; knock, and it will be opened to you. For everyone who asks receives, and he who seeks finds, and to him who knocks it will be opened." As she closed her Bible, she commented simply, "I have found this to be true." In my embattled soul I vowed, "If that woman comes back to class, I will not attend." I later learned that Nancy regularly took care of the nursery and so my prayer was answered. She did not return.

One elderly couple was very kind in seeking to mentor me. The wife loaned me a book to read: The Burden Is Light by Eugenia Price. In Eugenia's description of her path to belief in Jesus Christ in her thirties, I began to see what was lacking in my own faith. When she met Jesus, everything in her life changed: her career, her view of life and other people, and her goals. I realized I had kept God in a box of my own making. I had never surrendered the control of my life to God.

One morning I got up with a sense of an impending decision needing to be made. Would I continue to live my life as I was or would I make a decision to give God the reins of my life? I was feeling my dilemma physically, my heart pounding in my chest. Into my mind came these words: "You need to make a decision. You have been here before and have let the opportunity pass. One day you will not hear the call anymore." I knew this was a pivotal moment in my life. My brother was a committed Christian and I valued his counsel. I decided to call him, but when his wife answered the phone,and I learned he was not at home, I asked her to pray for me to turn my life over to God.

She seemed surprised and questioned, "Do you mean you're not a Christian?" I knew in my heart I was a Christian but I now needed to take an additional step and let God have control. As she promised to pray for me, I hung up the phone, and knew that by asking for prayer, I had, indeed, decided to give my life completely to God.

To make this decision official, I prayed, "God, if you are there, I give You my life. It's not worth much, but if You want it, it's Yours."

I had reached the end of self. Broken and willing to have God take over, I now surrendered myself to Him.

I sensed immediately something had shifted inside of me. When I looked out the window at the spring day, the colors were more vivid. I *knew* God had reached down to enfold me and graciously turn me around in a new direction. "How can this happen, God," I asked, "when I don't even know who Jesus is?" His mercy amazed me.

The answer sounded softly in my spirit, "I will teach you." Sometime later I read that Jesus promises in John 15:26: "But I will send you the Comforter—the Holy Spirit, the source of all truth. He will come to you from the Father and will tell you all about me." (Living Bible) Another prompting came into my spirit, "Nancy will teach you." The woman whose presence I had so detested in the Sunday School class, was actually the person God sent to teach me. The enemy had certainly tried to keep me from that help.

That next Sunday I was late to church, and who was also waiting to go into the sanctuary? *Nancy*. As we stood waiting, I quickly told her I had given my life into God's hands and the Holy Spirit told me I should ask her to teach me. She seemed to accept my statement with approval. As I sat beside her in church that Sunday, we both felt the blessing of God on our friendship as we realized the sermon that morning was from chapter 3 of John chronicling Nicodemus's visit to Jesus where he learned what it means to be "born again."

Over the next several months Nancy came frequently to my home. Together we looked for answers to my questions in the Bible. With my surrender to God had come a new-born faith. Not only did I believe everything the Bible taught, but I felt God's love surrounding me and His Spirit quickening the Truth to me.

Nancy had a large family with children of all ages. When my children and I visited her family, I marveled at how polite and self-disciplined the children were. They listened to their parents obediently and treated one another with kindness. One day I commented on this, and said, "Would you help me with parenting my children?"

She laughed, amused, "I thought you would never ask!" She gave me literature to read and mentored me in the care of my home as well as helping me to understand the need for consistent rules for my children. I could not get over how peaceful my home became.

I learned Nancy was part of a group of people in the church who believed in the Gifts of the Spirit, including healing, miracles, and praying in the Spirit. The "something more" I so yearned for, began to unfold in our study of the Scriptures, especially the book of Acts. Now I not only believed with childlike faith everything I read of the supernatural power of God, but I began to experience that power working in my own life. When I was sick, I prayed for healing, fully expecting God to answer my prayer, and He did. Our extended family agreed to pray every day at noon to ask God to set my father free of alcoholism, and within a year, he was delivered and began a new life. When my children were sick, I laid hands on them and prayed and saw them recover.

I learned from Brother Lawrence's book The Practice of the Presence to pray about everything: what I would serve for dinner, what flowers to send to a friend's mother's funeral ("How did you know her favorite was yellow roses?" her daughter asked.), and decisions I needed to make. As I yielded my will to God, I sensed His guidance in every aspect of my life. My husband had attended church only sporadically, but now we changed churches to one of a denomination familiar to him, and he became active, ordained as a deacon.

It was the 1970s and there was a movement of the Holy Spirit sweeping the country. In the Washington, D.C. area where we currently lived, it was especially prevalent. Nancy and another friend from the Sunday School class, Alice, took me to Catholic prayer groups, Lutheran meetings, and ecumenical Bible studies. As music played, people worshipped the Lord with hands up-raised, something I had started to do instinctively in my private prayer times. What a surprise to see that practice mirrored in public meetings.

That summer I visited my parents in Michigan, and I was so full of joy that I could not help but share with them how God had changed my life. My father was skeptical. I realized what would convince him: from the time I was a child I had sucked my thumb. As I grew older, my parents tried every way they could think of to motivate me to quit. But when I needed reassurance in the pages of a book, or help going to sleep, I would unconsciously find my thumb in my mouth. When I went to college, God supplied special roommates who never mocked or shamed me about this habit. Dad had said, "What are you going to do when you get married?" but here again God supplied a husband who was kind to me and never made fun of me. When God touched my life in that Spring of 1971, I was thirty-one, and I was in awe that a supernatural God had reached down to redeem me. I prayed, "God, as sign that you have changed me, please take away the desire to suck my thumb." I was conscious that God had reached deep inside my heart and given me the reassurance I had always lacked. So, that summer day, I looked with wonder at my dad and said, "Daddy, I asked God to take away the desire to suck my thumb, and it is gone!" What precious and welcome proof this was to my doubting father.

I have never been sorry I turned my life over to God. He is faithful to care for me, guide me, and patient in seeking to teach me His ways. He promises to never leave me or forsake me. (Hebrews 13:5) To be sure, there are times I struggle. I love the picture in Matthew 8:23-26 of the disciples in a boat fearfully facing a storm, beside themselves with worry that they are going to perish. Meanwhile, Jesus is unperturbed, sound asleep in the boat. I am often like those disciples, and Jesus says to me, as He did to them, "You of little faith, why are you so afraid?" And then He calms the storm. When I turn to Jesus and allow Him to take control, He brings me peace.

If you are in that place of wanting something more out of life—of seeking purpose—surrender your life to Jesus as Lord of your life. You will never be sorry. Philippians 4:19 says, "And my God will meet all your needs according to His glorious riches in Christ Jesus."

In Germany kneeling on the cellar floor I had prayed, "God, I want more of this love, whatever it is." I have learned that this Love is Jesus, who loved us so much that he died on a cross to take away our sins and bring us into the family of God. I know now He rose again so that after death we might live for all eternity with Him and the Father in heaven. If you want to place your life in His hands, He is waiting. Don't delay, because the day may come, when you will no longer hear God's pleading voice. I Corinthians 6:3 says, "Behold, *now* is the day of salvation." You'll never be sorry you made the decision to entrust your life to Jesus. He'll become your best Friend.

During the years 1975 until 1996 on Thursday nights, there was a small group of people that met together in the home of Lucile Trout, in rural Nokesville, Virginia. The following stories come from three women who were members of that prayer group.

10

The Comfort of His Presence – Excerpts from the Journals of Lucile Wilson Trout

Lucile Wilson Trout wrote in her memoirs for her family, "This old world has changed so much since I first saw the light of day on January 20, 1909. So many things that were a part of our lives in the early days have disappeared from the face of the earth and our children and grandchildren would never know them." She remembers taking baths in the kitchen in a round galvanized tin washtub, people running out of their houses to see an airplane passing in the sky overhead, and her home with gas lights, a gas stove, and a coal furnace.

Lucile was four years old when her father, who worked for The Bureau of Pensions of the Department of Interior, was transferred from Knoxville, Tennessee to Washington, D.C. In Washington she remembered "a little Italian man with a long stick would come around every evening about twilight and light the (gas) lamps on posts. In the early mornings he would come and shut them off. I can remember standing on our porch and watching the fire wagons with their white horses and clanging bells tearing down Tennessee Avenue. About once a year the Barnum and Bailey Circus would come to town. It came from Union Station down B Street, N.E. and then Tennessee Avenue to 15th and H. The principal of the school would send two boys out to watch for the parade. When they would sight the parade a way off, they would run in and report it and the whole school would be let out to sit on the curb and watch the parade. There would be elephants, clowns, music, bears, lions in cages, and monkeys."

Lucile remembered walking the three blocks to Eastern Presbyterian Church at 6th and C Streets, N.E. "At age four I was in the Beginners Class. The song 'Jesus Loves Me' in that class made an impression on me that has lasted all these many years. As a child, Jesus put a desire in my heart to become a missionary."

However, Lucile was sickly as a child, diagnosed with gastritis. She writes, "I couldn't eat sweets, fruit, or hot breads—in fact, I couldn't eat anything I liked and hated everything I *could* eat, like spinach, kale, etc. I also had a heart condition and was not supposed to jump rope or run up steps. I had to miss all of the first semester of the second grade. In the fourth grade our class went to the museum and I had to stay in another classroom because the trip would be too much for me. I really don't ever remember complaining about any of these things or feeling sorry for myself. I would even go to the store with the other children. They would buy a penny's worth of candy, offer me some, and I would not eat any. I had more discipline then than I do now."

When Lucile was nine years old, she had her tonsils taken out and from then on, she began to grow stronger. "By eighth grade I could eat normally, and in high school I was allowed to take physical education and do whatever the other children did.

"When I was seventeen in 1926, I attended a youth conference at Hood College in Frederick, Maryland. The last night of the conference I committed my life to full time service for Christ. I remember going to bed that night and weeping uncontrollably. I can't remember why I was crying, but I believe God touched my life that night."

"Now the sad part," she writes. "When I returned home, and told my father about it, he quenched the Spirit and told me it was an emotional reaction. (He did not want me to be a missionary.) I accepted his counsel and believed that I had been taken advantage of emotionally and from that time on I believe Satan had a hold on me. There was certainly a war going on in my spirit. I believe, however, that God provided a covering to protect me. As I write this I can look back and see that disobedience to the Holy Spirit brings suffering and heartache."

Although her parents disapproved, Lucile married Athey Trout on January 20, 1937. This would be a difficult marriage, but in the end, God answered many prayers for the couple.

As regarding Lucile's call to be a missionary, years later God would show Lucile that she had fulfilled that call. Each day of the week throughout her life she prayed for a different part of the world, and interceded for the needs of missionaries with whom she became acquainted. Here are some of the entries in Lucile's journal of answers to prayer.

January, 1975 – Lucile knew the Father and Jesus but she knew nothing about the Holy Spirit. After being in a meeting at a Catholic church with mostly college students home on break, her heart was open to receive what was mentioned in the meeting as "The Baptism of the Holy Spirit." At that meeting she heard young people giving their testimonies, sharing their blessings and their needs; they sang "in the Spirit" and a prophecy was given that encouraged everyone there. Lucile read books by Catherine Marshall (perhaps: *The Helper* and *Something More*) and Dennis Bennett (*Eight O'clock in the Morning*) and began to understand that there was another dimension to the Christian faith.

She wrote: "I went to Jesus in my bedroom one afternoon and asked forgiveness for every sin I could remember, and forgave everyone I could think of that I had ever held anything against – and asked for the Baptism in the Holy Spirit."

In her thoughts Jesus answered very clearly, "What are you going to do about the trash man?"

"I answered out loud, 'What do you mean, the trash man? I don't know any trash man.' Then 'Oh!...Oooh!...Ooooh!' Our neighbors across the road had a trash man and we were putting our trash with theirs and paying them every other month. The trash man was being 'beat' out of one patron. I immediately picked up the phone and called our neighbor and told her we would like to have our trash picked up on our side of the road, and asked her, 'Who is the trash man?' Then I phoned him and arranged for him to pick up our trash. The Holy Spirit was beginning to convict me and cleanse me of the *trash* in my life.

"Soon after that the Lord began telling me to stop playing Bridge. I had been praying Bridge for over thirty years and I argued with Him for nearly a year. I told Him that it was the only fun that I had and I never let Bridge interfere with my church work. But He would say one word 'Bridge.' Bridge began to turn sour, I was not enjoying it, but I still did not obey. Finally, one morning at an Aglow meeting, the speaker asked us to stand and let go of anything that was separating us from God. And He (the Lord) said loud and clear in my heart 'BRIDGE,' and I said, 'Okay, Father, I give up, You win.'

I went home and called my Bridge friends and asked them to get someone to take my place. They couldn't believe He meant it. But it was the easiest thing I ever did. I have never since had the slightest desire to play Bridge. Not that it was wrong, but it was wrong for me. And I learned that when we obey Him, He makes it easy to do."

Lucile read the book *They Speak with Other Tongues* by John Sherrill, explaining about the gift of tongues (1 Corinthians 12:10). In the meeting with the college students Lucile had heard about this gift and had heard people worshipping in languages she could not understand. She told her daughter, Dorothy, "I don't need those tongues."

"But a few months later I began to say to myself, 'Everybody else (in the charismatic meetings) has tongues – I'd like to have them too.' Then I asked God for a prayer language and it came, but at first, I thought I was doing it myself – it took a while for me to believe it was real.

"Some few months after receiving the Baptism in 1975, the Lord brought together a small group that met on Thursday nights. At one meeting I asked for the laying on of hands and prayer for release from fear. I had all my life been afraid of the dark. That very night fear left me. Another night I asked for release from resentment and God took out of my heart the resentment I had lived with for many years. Then He showed me the verse, "Great peace have they that love Thy law, and *nothing shall offend them." Psalm 119:165 - KJV*. I keep ahold of that verse. I refuse to be offended. At least I try."

"(Another entry) I have three little folding stools with red cloth seats. They are very light and I take them to parades and to the yard and garden when I am working there, to rest when I get tired. The seat on the third stool broke last summer and Athey and I have tried to figure a way to replace the seats. There seemed no way unless he took out some of the rivets. I said, 'Jesus, there must be a way to repair these stools and You know how to do it.' Before the words were out of my mouth, He told me exactly how to do it, and they were better than the originals, so that I can slip them off and wash them. Praise the Lord! 'You do not have because you do not ask.' (James 4:2b - KJV)

July 23, 1981. "I picked lima beans last evening and weeded as I picked. When I went to bed last night the back of my right hand was red and slightly swollen. It felt like it was on fire—very painful. I had read that morning and underlined Psalm 107:20 KJV, 'He sent His Word and healed them... .' I prayed this over and over, adding, 'Lord, I believe—help Thou mine unbelief.' I went to sleep. This morning my hand is slightly sore, but *healed*. Praise You, Jesus!

"On Thanksgiving Day, November 26, 1981, we had dinner at Dorothy's. Before leaving for home, I was led to phone Harry Daniels in D.C. Grace, his wife, had been ill. When Harry answered he was more or less in a state of panic. Grace was having trouble with her colostomy and he didn't know what to do and couldn't get a doctor because of the holiday. I told him that Dorothy and I would pray and ask God to send help or tell him what to do. Though Harry and Grace are not Christians, he was relieved to know that we would pray.

"Dorothy and I did pray immediately and asked God to help them. We learned later that right after I called, probably while Dorothy and I were praying, whatever was wrong with the colostomy was corrected and everything was all right. '...before they call, I will answer; and while they are yet speaking, I will hear.' (Isaiah 65:24 - KJV)

That evening I asked for a scripture and He gave me Isaiah 50:2,4 - KJV: 'Is my hand shortened at all, that it cannot redeem? Or have I no power to deliver? The Lord God hath given me the tongue of the learned that I should know how to speak a word in season to him that is weary.' Praise Him! I will make this scripture a part of me and God will bless it."

As is already apparent, Lucile prayed about everything for which she needed help. The next entry is called, "The Miracle of the Cows."

"Thursday May 20, 1982, 9:00 am. A good day to set out the plants my husband had been nurturing under grow-lights in the basement for many weeks. A light rain the night before had softened the ground for planting. Over near the pasture, just beyond two rows of asparagus, we set out fifty cantaloupe plants. We noted that the two rows of strawberries on the other side of the asparagus were blooming bountifully and the berries would be ready to pick very shortly.

"In another garden back of the barn, we set out twenty tomato plants and planted a row of snap beans. My scarlet sage and impatiens were tenderly placed in beds on the side of the house and below the kitchen window on the east. We spoke to 'Minnie', the little blue fir tree given to us when we visited friends in Minnie-sota and told her how pretty she looked. She was growing near the bed of peonies in the front of the house and just beyond a bed of day-lilies and phlox, which were beginning to bud. Praise God for the beauty of His bounty! That morning, as every morning in our devotions, we asked God to bless and protect our little farm and guide us as to His will for it and for us as we grow older.

"That evening, May 20th 9:00 PM our little Thursday evening prayer and praise group was gathered in our living room—six of us this night. During the years we had been meeting, many prayers had been answered, some miraculously. (During the Prayer Meeting) Our neighbor's herd of cattle had pushed through the fence and were having a hey-day all over our gardens, lawn, driveway, front yard, back yard—everywhere! Some were in the road in front of the house.

"A quick phone call brought the neighbor and his helpers, with my husband, to the scene of the intrusion. Our little group immediately went into prayer, each of us in turn praying aloud in our own way that the cows would be restored to their pasture without harm to them or to us, also that there would be no angry feelings as a result of the damage done. Within an hour nearly a hundred cows had been retrieved and returned to pasture and to safety.

"The morning after at 8:00 AM a survey of the farm to observe the destruction. Hoof prints several inches deep almost solid *between* the rows of strawberries. The tops of a very small section of one row had been eaten. The rest of the blooms were untouched! Hoof prints and big blobs of cow dung *between* the rows of asparagus. Asparagus untouched! Hoof prints beside 'Minnie' the little fir tree. 'Minnie' untouched! Prints alongside the flower beds, in the tomato plants. Only four tomato plants mashed down. The Snap beans' planting—prints alongside but not on it. No need to replant. Scarlet sage, impatiens, peonies, phlox and day-lilies untouched.

"10:00 AM – Phone call from the wife of the dairy farmer, apologizing profusely for the damage done—their insurance agent would be out in the afternoon to estimate the damage. Reply: No damage—no need for an estimate. We *pray* for this farm!

"March 5, 1983. What a beautiful beginning for a trip! I spent the last night at Dorothy's and Tony's to await (the others) to go to Saranac Lake, New York, to the North Country Christian Center. When I walked into the kitchen at 5:00 AM, there on the table on two cooling racks were dozens of large chocolate cookies, and a note propped up between the racks.

" 'Grandmother, have a nice trip!' Matthew, age nine, had gotten up in the middle of the night and made cookies as a going-away gift for me. I believe that was the sweetest gift anyone has ever given me. 'But Jesus said, Let the little children come to Me and do not forbid them; for of such is the kingdom of heaven.' Matthew 19:14.

"December 14, 1983. Last night I put the tape of Efrem Zimbalist, Junior's reading of Psalms 70 – 102 on my tape recorder and while listening, I fell asleep. I dreamt that Pat Robertson (700 Club) had set a table. I saw him spreading a table cloth on a round table. There were platters of meat cut in one-inch cubes. Dorothy was sitting on my left and some man on my right. We were gorging ourselves on this meat, which was tender and delicious. No matter how much we ate, we could not get enough. It was *so good.* In the meantime, Pat was reciting Scripture and I remember thinking, 'Pat must know the whole Bible by heart.' (No doubt I was hearing the Psalms that Efrem Zimbalist was reading.) It came to me that the meat we were eating was the Word of God and that was why it was so delicious and we couldn't get enough, no matter how much we ate.

"July 1984. Something has been eating and destroying our sweet corn, so I asked the Lord, in our breakfast devotions, to move these little animals elsewhere, and sure enough there have been no more animals in our corn. But the night of August 2nd, while our prayer group was meeting, Athey had a call from a neighbor telling him that *his* corn was being eaten by varmints. Could I have prayed them up the road?

"November 29, 1984. Several years ago, the Lord put it on my heart to pray for Robert Mugabe, president of Zimbabwe (formerly Rhodesia) and for the healing of that land. I have been lifting him up in prayer regularly, asking that he be convicted of his sins, brought to repentance and receive salvation. I kept reminding the Lord that I was standing in the gap for Mugabe, believing I was the only one praying for him. Yesterday on the 700 Club, Franklin Graham told Pat Robertson that a missionary had led Mugabe's wife to Jesus; that many people have been praying for Mugabe."

Lucile wrote that on Wednesday, July 23, 1985 about 5:00 PM, a caller from the 700 Club, a Christian television program, called.

Lucile had also volunteered herself as a caller for this ministry for many years, praying with people who called in. On this evening when the caller asked if Lucile had a prayer request, she did. "I asked that he pray that my husband be released from the bondage of alcohol. I believe the caller said his name was Roger. I wish I could contact him and let him know how his prayer was answered.

"The following Sunday, July 27th, we planned a family dinner to celebrate Athey's eightieth birthday. That Saturday, in the middle of the night, Athey awoke, got out of bed, and tried to get to the bathroom. He was so dizzy and sick he couldn't walk or even get back in bed. I put pillows on the floor beside the bed and kept cold cloths on his head all night. Sunday morning he managed to get back into bed but couldn't raise his head off the pillow. He had never in his life been so sick. He said, 'It must have been the sandwich I ate.'"

"The family began arriving after church and Tony (Athey's son-in-law) went upstairs to see him. He came back down elated. Athey had said three times that he would never take another drink as long as he lived. I am rewriting this in March of '88 and am praising the Lord that Athey had no problem whatsoever in stopping drinking. Jesus just took away the desire."

During the intervening years Athey made many trips to the Emergency Room and the hospital. Several times Lucile and her prayer group prayed him through life-threatening crises. December 5th of 1985 Athey went to the hospital with terrible pains in his abdomen, but after removing his appendix he seemed to improve. The following night the hospital staff called Lucile to tell her that a sonogram showed an aneurysm in the aorta. The surgery was to be performed immediately, and the chances of his survival were slim. Lucile called her prayer group to pray through the night, while Athey continued to battle for his life.

"Two nights later, Athey's sister and her husband from Earleysville, Virginia, ... had been to see him and stopped by the house to tell me he was very restless, hallucinating, taking tubes out and trying to get out of bed. He begged them to take him home. He had said, 'I beseech you on bended knee to get me out of this place.' So, I sent Tony who went in at midnight and stayed with him until nine o'clock the next morning.

When I arrived that morning, Tony was ecstatic. He said they had talked about fishing and gardening, and all sorts of things. Athey had said to him, "I've been praying constantly ever since I've been here. I know I am a sinner, but Jesus has forgiven my sins."

The Nokesville rescue squad brought Athey home on Christmas Eve but he was in a great deal of pain. Five days later they returned him to the hospital and diagnosed him with gastritis. On January 2nd he returned home but developed pneumonia. This time his doctor thought it best to treat him at home. Lucile writes, "I had to give him medicine through the night. One night he was having the strangest dream. He saw a pile of Christmas packages, gift wrapped, all the same size, and he was opening them. Inside were bones and body parts and he was thanking the Lord for them."

To Lucile this brought to mind the Scripture in Ezekial 37:4b – 14 - KJV: "O ye dry bones, hear the word of the Lord. Thus saith the Lord God unto these bones; Behold I will cause breath to enter into you, and ye shall live: And I will lay sinews upon you, and will bring up flesh upon you, and cover you with skin, and put breath in you, and ye shall live: and ye shall know that I am the Lord."

Following this period of grave illness, Lucile writes," As for Athey, recovery seemed slow to him, but it really wasn't. When spring came, he was able to plant his garden and continue remodeling the house. Gradually he has improved to where he can do just about anything he wants. Best of all, he is a new creature in Christ Jesus. 'Therefore if any man be in Christ, he is a new creature: old things are passed away; behold all things are become new.' II Corinthians 5:17 -KJV."

"October 12, 1987. Fred (her son) left last night to drive to Oxford, Mississippi, about a twenty-hour trip and I was concerned that he might get tired and go to sleep while driving. I asked the Lord to send His angels and keep him awake and give him a safe trip. Fred phoned at 6:30 this evening to let me know he had arrived safely. He said he got as far as Memphis, and he got lost and the car started driving strangely. He 'just happened' to be passing a Sears store so he stopped and had them fix the car—the wheels needed aligning and it took about two hours to fix them. Thank You, Jesus, for giving him those two hours rest from driving and bringing him safely to his destination.

"February 2, 1989, my friend, Ken Starr, told me this story: 'Several years ago I was surf fishing at Emerald Isle, North Carolina. Walking down the beach, I picked up some small shells and said aloud that I would like to find a really big beautiful shell. Going back to fishing I threw my line out and it caught something so heavy it was hard to pull in. It was a large beautiful shell filled with sand. It had probably been buried under the sand for years.'"

"March 1990. Wycliffe Bible translators Jon and Carolyn Miller have been on my prayer list since before the Vietnam War ended and they were captured by the Vietnamese. They are free in Malaysia now and send me personal air letters which include specific prayer requests. I mark the prayer requests in red and each morning in my devotions I spread out these letters before the Lord and agree with Jon and Carolyn in asking that these requests be granted. There is no distance in the Spirit.

"Their February letter arrived early in March and after reading it, for some reason I threw it in the trash along with a lot of other mail that came that morning. That afternoon, Athey burned the trash.

The next morning, as I lifted the letters before the Lord, I asked His forgiveness for destroying the one that had just come. But there was no way I could retrieve it. The trash had been burned.

"I went downstairs to fix breakfast and open up the house. I went out on the porch and couldn't believe my eyes. The letter was by the outside door, all by itself, perfectly clean, waiting to be picked up. My first thought was that Athey must have dropped it when he took the trash out, but he takes the whole basket out, and he did not know anything about it. And it was not there when I locked the door the night before. *God wanted me to pray over that letter.*

"In September of 1991, God impressed Tony that he should send $500.00 to a minister who was starting a new church in Vermont. The next morning Tony told Dorothy he felt he should send this minister some money, would she pray about it? That evening she said she felt they should do so. Tony asked how much should they send, and her answer was, "How about $500.00?" Tony felt they should send it right away and they did. The minister wrote back that he had been looking for a place to live and had come up with a place for a $500 lease but had not signed it. Tony's check arrived and he signed the lease. Since that time Tony received a bonus from his job of $1,250.

"It's January 23, 1992 – prayer group meeting tonight. It rained hard all morning. Athey and I went to Manassas for groceries and lunch. We could hardly see to drive. After putting the groceries away, I went upstairs to take a nap. On the way up I spoke to Jesus about the meeting tonight. I said, 'Jesus, this is your meeting, not mine. If you want us to have it, You can take care of the weather. You could even make the sun come out if You wanted to.' I slept hard for over an hour and was wakened with the sun shining in my face. The weather cleared and we had a wonderful meeting. Jesus was very present with us. He is so good!"

Lucile Trout died in February of 1996 and her husband was heartbroken. Her daughter, Dorothy, writes, "But she had told him he wouldn't die until he had given his heart to Jesus. (He didn't go to church, so perhaps she wanted to be SURE!) Thus, he became a man on a mission with his first phone call being to Mom's pastor! He worked hard getting the house cleaned out and straightening out old wrongs. On a shopping day in Manassas, Dad spotted Freddie (his son) and we followed him into a parking lot. Dad talked to him as he got out of his car, asking Freddie for forgiveness. The response was not good, but Dad knew he had done all he could. He met with the pastor again in the fall. It was as if he knew the time was short. He reaffirmed his commitment to the Lord.

"Daddy stayed at the old homestead as long as he was able, but in November he moved in with Tony and me, unable to safely maneuver the stairs any longer.

Ten days later, on December 4, he sat down to the dinner table with me to have some pie. Once again, he said, 'When do you think the Lord will let me go home to be with Mama?'

I replied, 'When He's ready, I guess,' I looked down and took a bite of pie. When I looked up, he was falling over out of the chair. I caught him and called for Tony. We called 911, but it was already over. God had said, 'It is time.'

"You might remember while Daddy was in the hospital some years ago, the Lord told him He had given him new body parts (the Christmas packages with body parts). He had been an alcoholic until he was eighty and had cancer of the rectum in 1989. Yet, Daddy died of old age, not sickness, and only when God called him home. God really did give him new body parts! Amazing.

"The tombstone for both Mom and Dad reads, 'New Address: Heaven.'"

11

Forgiven and Redeemed! Pam's Story

The stores were decorated in bright colors and Christmas carols echoed from loud speakers. The scent of pine boughs was in the air, and strings of lights lit up the dark streets all over town. It was December, a month bringing excitement as people planned for the holidays. For Pam it was a month that brought back a memory loaded with guilt, bringing on depression. Pam had cried until she thought there were no tears left.

The first tears came when she awoke from the anesthetic and realized the baby was gone. Immediately, a darkness settled over her spirit. She knew she had made a terrible mistake. "It was my own decision," she told herself. "I will just have to live with it."

She had been in nursing school when she met her husband, Jim, a policeman. Quiet and deep, with sandy hair, at six feet four inches, he towered over Pam's five feet seven. She remembered saying to herself, "This is someone for me." When they married in 1966, they both agreed they only wanted two children. Their daughter was born eleven months later.

Pam's parents chided them, "We thought you were going to wait awhile and have fun as a couple."

But Pam says, "We were excited and happy, because we wanted children." Pam was one of four siblings; she loved babysitting all through her teen years, and teaching children's Sunday school. Their daughter was a year and a half, when Pam and Jim decided to try to have another child. Pam soon discovered she was pregnant, and she talked it over with God. "I told God, 'we have a daughter now and I only want two kids, two's enough in this world. We would love to have a boy, and we thank You if You could do that for us.' I think I was making a deal with God, which you're not supposed to do. I don't know if those were my exact words but that was my intent.

"So, He blessed us! We had a son in 1970. We had two children and we were happy. But also, I wanted to make that a firm decision, that we wouldn't have any more kids." When Pam asked to be sterilized, her doctors said she was too young to be limiting herself—she was twenty-three—and she had only two children. Jim was told a similar thing about having a vasectomy. "I didn't know if that was a law, but it must have been or they wouldn't have told me that," Pam recalls. "I didn't understand, and it didn't register in my brain very well."

The young couple tried to be careful, but in the fall of the following year Pam found out she was pregnant for the third time. She used a test to be sure, and when the results were verified, she was distraught. "I didn't really want to be pregnant, but what could I do?"

"That set me off on a bad path," Pam says. "I didn't talk to my minister or any family members to get advice. I can look back and see it more realistically than at the time it happened. To my selfish mindset at that moment, another child seemed like a great interruption of my life plan, and I thought two children were all I could handle as a young mother."

She had two gynecologists, one Methodist and one Catholic. She knew the Catholic doctor would not give her the advice she wanted, so she went to the other doctor. She told him she knew she was pregnant and she did not want another child. "Instead of urging me to carry the baby the doctor said, 'This is the only way we can do this.' He called it a therapeutic D & C." With hind sight Pam realizes what a difference it would have made had she gone to the Catholic doctor. "He probably would have encouraged me and said, 'This is what you need to do. How can I help you?'"

This was 1971 and there were laws about how early an abortion could be done. Pam figured she was nine weeks pregnant so the doctor urged her to go to the hospital and have the procedure done quickly. Pam anguished over the situation. "I prayed and cried, and asked God to stop the surgery if He didn't want me to go through with it. God gives us free will and He allows us to make our own choices, even when they are against His Word, and even when we are wrong! Right after I woke up from the abortion, I knew I had made a mistake," Pam says. "*I felt that in my whole being.*"

"When I came home from the hospital, something passed into the toilet. I looked at it, picked it out of the toilet. It looked like a body part, an arm or leg but without a hand or foot attached. It was awful. I could have died. It really shook me."

She called the gynecologist and he said, "Oh, I know. That's probably nothing. Don't worry about it. It was so early. That was just a clump of cells, a little tissue, don't worry about that."

Pam was convinced it wasn't just a clump of cells but a baby. How small or how big was it? She wasn't even sure when she got pregnant. "*Oh my gosh, this is not good,*" she told herself. "I felt a deep sadness, sorrow and regret. Why didn't someone stop this? I prayed for God's forgiveness."

Years later, when she saw drawings, pictures, and models of babies so that you could visualize the size of the child at certain weeks, this confirmed her original response: there had been a baby in her womb. In addition, research would show that babies feel pain and have a heartbeat *very early*. "All the things I learned were good for me to learn, but that just re-affirmed what a terrible mistake I had made, and it hit me like a ton of bricks." At some point Pam did not cry anymore, but she felt a terrible sadness that never left. While she knew God had forgiven her, she could not forgive herself.

Because of her guilt over this loss, Pam began to think the solution was to have another baby. She thought that might help her to heal and relieve the crying spells. However, things had changed and Jim had been able to have a vasectomy. Pam moaned, "Everyone is having babies," but the couple knew it was final, there would not be any more children. Pam says, "Frustrations escalated, tensions grew, but life went on even though laced with suppressed depression and feelings of worthlessness." The couple worked at putting their disappointment behind them.

Her embarrassment and shame only increased when in 1973 the national discussion of abortion intensified around the case of Roe v. Wade. Pam had not told anyone about the abortion. "I felt that if people knew what I had done, they would look down on me. At times I felt like a murderer. I found comfort in reading in the Bible in Isaiah 1:18, 'Come now and let us reason together,' says the Lord. 'Though your sins are like scarlet, they shall be as white as snow, though they are red like crimson, they shall be as wool.' "

She and Jim often discussed what had happened. They both knew the day would come when they would need to tell their children, but the timing never seemed exactly right. "I was sick about it. They were little at the time, but even as they became teenagers, I just couldn't." In 1997 their daughter came to tell them she was pregnant. She was thirty years old, had been out on her own, had a college degree and was teaching. Pam says, "She and I went into the bedroom and sat and cried when she told me. And I almost told her right then what had happened to me, but I didn't. She planned on carrying the child even if the father refused to marry her. She was financially able to care for herself and the child. 'I thank God,' I told her, 'and I am so proud of you.' And we had a wonderful time together. That same year she and the father of the child married. So that's our oldest grandchild."

At the same time, their son and his wife announced they were expecting their first child. Then, sadly she lost the baby. Their daughter was having problems as well. After she had her baby, she and her husband began having marital problems. Their daughter was going to counseling but it looked like they would divorce.

In her spirit Pam had felt for some time that God was telling her she would know when it was time to share with her children that she had had an abortion, and now in 1998, she knew she *had* to have that conversation. "I shared and opened up with each one separately, because they didn't live near-by. It was a very sensitive situation. My husband was with me, but I did all the talking. It was wonderful that the timing was right."

"My son and his wife lived together before they married. His wife had a life before him that we knew nothing about. In this conversation we learned she had given up a child for adoption. And there was my daughter finding out she was pregnant before marriage. It's amazing how everything happened the way it did. My son and daughter-in-law were understanding. We had a lot to share and they both did. My children had the attitude, 'If it weren't for the grace of God, there go we.' They all expressed their forgiveness to me. I was very thankful for that. That was the thing that bothered me most: I had thought, 'How could anyone forgive me for doing that?' "

Underlying Pam's life all these years was a feeling that she wanted to help other women who were struggling with an unwanted or unexpected pregnancy. She thought helping them might also help her to heal. In 2001 Pam heard about the Crisis Pregnancy Center of a ministry called Care Net. She and Jim had moved from Maryland to Virginia and in their new church there was a presentation with booklets detailing how the Center helped people who had had abortions while also offering assistance to women who were pregnant. "I went in to Care Net to volunteer, but I found out that I first had to admit I had had an abortion. Before I could counsel others, I had to go through a Bible study by Linda Cohrane called *Forgiven and Set Free.*

That was a wonderful program," Pam says. The course lasted several months. One of the leaders had been through the Bible study herself after her abortion, and was able to share with the women the freedom and forgiveness she had received from God. The other leader was a trained counselor. As people went through the Bible study they learned about God's character and discussed their relationship with Him. They shared with one another about their experience of having an abortion.

They used a pie chart to show the names of all the people who were responsible for this decision. Pam had always taken all the guilt on herself. "Initially it was me, me, me. I took the blame for everything. But when I listened and read more, I tried to figure it out: My husband knew; why didn't he stop me? My parents knew something; they had babysat for our children when I went to the hospital. The doctor, he's supposed to save lives. Why did he do the procedure? I was finally able to accept that other people shared responsibility for what had happened.

"Towards the end of the Bible study, we had the opportunity to name our baby, or babies—some people had had more than one abortion. Our leaders said God would lead us to name the baby. I did not even know the sex of my child, but as the weeks went by, a name came to me. It wasn't really a name but a nickname—letters: P.J. for Pam and Jim."

At the end of the Bible study course there was a memorial service. It was held in a small, ornate Episcopal Church. As Pam and the others who had finished the course entered the sanctuary, the fading light of day touched the colors from the stained-glass windows, dimly lighting the aisles and worn carpet between the dark wooden pews with their carvings. The walls of the sanctuary were decorated with oil paintings depicting Bible stories. Pam was conscious of music softly playing, giving a feeling of comfort and healing. They were led to the intimate space at the side of the altar, seated in the pews where the choir usually sat. The counselors who had directed the course faced them, leading the service.

"My husband came with me. He did not attend the Bible study but he knew all about it, had read the material, and supported me. Each of those participating could write a note to their baby. I just wrote a little something about how sorry I was that I had allowed this to take place in my life. 'And I don't know you yet, little baby, but I will someday. I believe God has forgiven me so I know that you are in God's arms, and with Jesus and the other children.'"

"One of the leaders had fashioned these little cloth dolls, that were representative of our baby. It had no face; it was just cotton with ties around it. It looked like a small angel a kid might make: the stuffed head, and a little body. We were sitting there in prayer with music playing. There were several songs that were just wonderful, relating to the subject of being forgiven. We were deep in our prayer, not paying attention to anything else, when one of the women handed me a doll, and said, 'This is your baby.' I took the doll in my hands. Suddenly there was this big gulp and there was a release of some big thing from inside of me. An eruption of emotion, I guess. I had never heard or felt anything like that before, totally involuntary on my part. At that moment God made me to know *I was forgiven; I was His child; He loved me; everything was going to be alright.*" The weight Pam had been carrying for many years—was finally gone.

"Pam turned to Jim and said, 'Honey, do you want to hold our baby?' Jim held the doll and the same thing happened to him. This eruption, with an actual noise, and afterward there was release, like a breath, a final 'let go'. At the end of the service, we carried the doll up to the front and put it in a basket draped with a cotton blanket, letting the baby go to the Lord."

Then Pam, Jim, and the others went outside where they were given balloons with a card on which a message could be written. There was a prayer and the balloons were let go into the air. Pam remembered the Scripture in Isaiah 43: 18, 19 that had come to mean so much to her through this process: "Forget the former things; do not dwell on the past. See, I am doing a new thing! Now it springs up; do you not perceive it? I am making a way in the desert and streams in the wasteland."

After completing the course, Pam and her husband began to volunteer at the Crisis Pregnancy Center sponsored by Care Net. Pam is a hugger, always smiling, and serving as a receptionist came naturally to her. She would greet women who came in, find out what they needed: a pregnancy test, were they married or single, how involved was the father willing to be, had they decided to carry the baby full term? She would find out if they went to church, and if they were open to it, Pam would pray with them. She encouraged them to trust God. She assured them that God had allowed this to happen and good could come from it. If they were seven to ten weeks pregnant, they could have a free ultra-sound. Pam says that once they heard the baby's heart beat on the ultra-sound, most were willing to carry the baby to term.

If there were problems of support, Pam informed the mothers of the services offered by the Pregnancy Center, and discussed the option of adoption. If they were willing to have the baby, a course was offered called "Ready on Arrival," using materials gathered by the facilitator of Care Net. By attending the course and in other ways, the women earned points which were then applied to acquiring cribs and other furniture and supplies for the baby. The center offered support all during pregnancy and after birth.

And as Pam, herself, had experienced, there was the course "Forgiven and Set Free" for women needing healing after an abortion. Pam was able to convince women and men, from her own experience, of God's forgiveness and the path to healing. Pam considered her volunteer work for Care Net a privilege.

Gradually, Pam realized that the loss of the baby was not only a loss for her and Jim, but her children had lost a brother or sister, her parents had lost a grandchild, her siblings had lost a niece or nephew. As Pam began to speak in public about her healing and forgiveness from God, she knew she needed to ask forgiveness from family members. When she apologized to her parents, "There was just my mom, dad, and me." Pam says, "It was very emotional but they never belittled me." All of this helped her family to heal as well. She was relieved to have the love and support of those who mattered most in her life.

Pam understands the tests we as humans go through. "No matter what the situation, I am responsible for what I do. I can't offer excuses for my sins. Instead, I acknowledge my guilt to God and accept the forgiveness He offers. (Psalm 32:5). That's the first step in exercising my individual responsibility. God has given me free will to make choices in my life, but I am accountable to God for my actions. I have a guardian angel because I *need* one. I've learned people are frail. When you read the Bible, you know what happened: Adam and Eve were kicked out of the Garden of Eden because they disobeyed. I have learned that obedience is so important, to be obedient to God's Word (the Bible) and what He is asking us to do, because we have accepted His offer of forgiveness and faith." She learned to trust God through the hard times. "I know He's never going to leave me, even though I trail off myself sometimes. He's always there. He's always available.

"There are so many Scriptures I just love. 'The joy of the Lord is my strength.' (Nehemiah 8:10) 'I can do all things through Christ who strengthens me.' (Philippians 4:13) There are plenty more, my Bible is full of markings. Certain Scriptures are important to me, and I feel God speaking to me (through them). I try to pass those on to everyone else, when I write cards."

Recently, her oldest grandson, twenty-one, wrote her a special note for Mothers' Day. "I wanted to write you some Scriptures too, Grandma, because you are always writing Scriptures to me." He had written Proverbs 31: 10 – 31, which begins: "A woman of noble character who can find? She is worth more than rubies." The chapter ends "Her children arise and call her blessed; her husband also, and he praises her: Many women do noble things, but you surpass them all. Charm is deceptive, and beauty is fleeting; but a woman who fears the Lord is to be praised. Give her the reward she has earned, and let her works bring her praise at the city gate."

12

Two Women – Yolanda "Yukie" Echols

> But Ruth replied (to her mother-in-law Naomi), "Don't urge me to leave you or to turn back from following you. Where you go I will go, and where you stay I will stay. Your people will be my people and your God my God. ... May the Lord deal with me, be it ever so severely, if anything but death separates you and me." Ruth 1: 16

The light breeze stirred Yukie Echols' hair as she sat on the porch with her head in her hands. Unaware of the scent of the Honeysuckle bush wafting on the gentle wind, Yukie concentrated on the prayer rising from her spirit. Every part of her body ached from rheumatoid arthritis. She could move only her eyes and her lips without pain; every other part of her body hurt whenever she moved. Yukie prayed, "Lord, there is no one in this world but You who knows the amount of pain I'm in. I don't know how to live or how to die. Lord, if this battle is almost over, please show me a beautiful bird."

Within two seconds Yukie heard a chirp rising from the throat of a tiny bird. Yukie looked up and saw a bird had landed on a fragile branch near her head. Yukie says, "It was beautiful! He looked right at me as he chirped. Then he flew away and came back again with another bird just like him, and the two of them sat on that small branch and chirped away, looking at me the whole time."

Yukie started to cry and seeing her tears, her mother-in-law, Mary, climbed down from the tractor mower and came over to see what was wrong. Yukie told her about her prayer and both women watched the birds. Mary loved birds and had bird books all over the place, but she had never seen this bird before.

From that day on Yukie knew she would be alright. She thought her healing was going to be instantaneous, but for a total of fifteen years she was totally dependent on someone to help her. She endured fifty-nine surgeries and twenty-two joint replacements. "And through it all I never had one infection," Yukie says, "so you know that's the Lord. Absolutely!" And during this time, her mother-in-law, Mary, took care of her.

Yukie laughs, "When my father-in-law died, Mary was fifty-nine and we moved her next door to us to take care of her, but she ended up taking care of me."

A short, strong woman, her greying hair cut in a bob, Yukie has a smile and a simple warmth that immediately draws people to her. Yukie met Don Echols at the city offices in Manassas, Virginia when she was nineteen. She was not romantically interested in her co-worker because he was married, but two years after his divorce, she and Don began to date. Don's mother, Mary, was not happy about the situation. Don had two children and Mary, a devout Christian, was praying for Don to reconcile with his wife. Meanwhile, Yukie helped Don's grandmother once a week with whatever she needed and took her to doctor's appointments.

Yukie says, "I was raised in the Appalachian Mountains of Kentucky. My dad was a coal miner and although he was not well educated, he had a lot of wisdom. We was raised in a coal mining camp. There were a lot of children in the camp and everybody helped one another. It was like one family."

Yukie's dad always sought people to help and taught his children by his example. "We were very poor, and I remember there would be people who didn't have anything to eat. My Dad'd come home and he'd half everything in the house to give away. He'd take us with him to deliver it around 2:00 in the morning, because they were proud people, even though they were poor. And we'd set it on their porch so they'd never know who helped.

"My mom would say, 'Lawson, what are our children going to eat tomorrow?'

"And he would say, 'Now, Ruby, everyone's going to eat today and God will take care of tomorrow.' "

If an elderly person needed things done, he would send his children to do it. "My dad would say God would bless us. We didn't know what a blessing was but it sounded good and we wanted it, so we would help. So as a child I think I had that in me."

Don's grandmother became very fond of Yukie. She told her daughter, Mary, "Please do right by Yukie because she will make Don a good wife."

Mary surrendered the situation to the Lord. She told Him, 'If this is the one, then just let it be.'"

After Yukie and Don married, they took care of his children every other weekend and a couple of nights during the week. Yukie says, "Don's two children were mostly with the mother. To this day I love them and they love me. Don and I were never able to have children—I lost three—so it all turned out really wonderful! Don has been an awesome husband. I could have searched the world over and never found someone better suited for me. So, I can see God's hand in all of it, from day one to the present."

As to her relationship with Don's mother, Yukie says there never was any tension between them and they became best friends. "When I came to know Mary, I was just so interested in how she lived her life and I wanted to be like that. When I was twelve, I remember sitting on a railroad track and giving my life to the Lord, but I didn't really live it until I met Mary. I went to a revival with her shortly after Don and I married and I knew that's what I wanted for the rest of my life."

"Then when I was thirty-four, I became ill with rheumatoid arthritis and eventually was bedridden and in a wheelchair. Mary took me to doctors and sought the Lord in prayer about what to do for me. She cut out all sugar and served me lots of fish and fresh vegetables. There was no medicine at first and everything was holistic. She cooked meals, she helped clean, and she encouraged me every day. She made me get up and move which is what I needed to do. She was there for everything I needed.

"I was in a lot of pain, oh, my goodness, yes. They told us that I should not lie down all the time because it would cause blood clots. Mary would urge me to move, but it was so incredibly painful, *truly*. I didn't know if I would ever be okay or not: ever be able to move again, to walk again, any of that."

To people going through intense and lengthy suffering, Yukie gives her prescription for avoiding depression and discouragement:

1. **"Keep your eyes on the Lord, look at what He's doing instead of what He's not doing or what you think He should do, and you can see Him every day in your life.** I just chose to do that. Going into surgery, I was always

looking at how it was going to be better. I expected good. Mary's friends would come by and keep me strong. Mary and I would pray together *every day*."

2. Yukie says **a daily time in the Word (The Bible) was the source of her strength.** She would read through the entire Bible every four and a half months. She also read over and over all of the Scriptures dealing with healing. A verse she especially loved was, "...the joy of the Lord is your strength." (Nehemiah 8:10). She says, "I figured if I kept joy, I would always have some strength. I had a wonderful family, a wonderful husband, and through it all I was truly blessed. God has supplied every need. I just figured God would never let me down. He said He wouldn't leave me or forsake me, and He never did!" (Hebrews 13:5)

3. Yukie says that **everyone can be useful, no matter what**. When she was bedridden and lamented that she couldn't work anymore, Mary told her she could be a prayer warrior. "People would call me and keep me busy all the time praying," Yukie says. Lucile Trout, a friend of Mary's, would keep a list of who she was praying for and mark them off as she heard the answers. Yukie started doing that. "It was a true blessing to do something."

Mary also encouraged Yukie to do counseling for the hospitals because she had gone through the replacements and surgeries so well. "With the attitude I had, I would talk to the patients before they went into surgery. Because I do believe healing is 50% attitude."

When she began to drive again, one of Yukie's doctors told her, "I have treated construction workers with fewer joint replacements and surgeries than you have had, who can't walk or drive. You are one amazing little woman!"

4. It helped that **Yukie was surrounded by positive people.** "I got to meet such wonderful people who believed and would encourage me, make me stronger. When I began to have problems and have all these surgeries my 'friends' disappeared. I remember asking the Lord, 'Why did you take every friend from me?' and He said, 'I didn't take them away from you; I took you away from them.' " The best friend of all, Yukie began to see, was God. "God took my friends away so my faith would not be in friends, but I would see what He was doing in my life."

5. Finally Yukie advises, "**Doctors can give you bad reports, but pray to see what God is telling you.** When you want a healing, seek the Healer, the Lord Jesus, and not the healing, because God's the One who knows how it's going to turn out; He knows what's best for you. Be ready to accept what God has for you. God used my arthritis to make Him everything in my life."

Yukie says her arthritis was probably the worst thing that happened to her but it was also the best thing. "I would not have known the Lord the way I do if he hadn't put me on my back. I didn't understand it at first—I was hurting and everything. It took me a couple of years to wrap my head around the fact that God would always be with me and in the end, it was going to be okay. It wasn't about me at all; it was about getting to know Him. We know of people, but often we don't really know them. I know of the President, but I don't really know him. And I believe that's how I felt about God."

And Mary was always there to care for her daughter-in-law. "I always told Mary, 'Someday I will take care of you.' She didn't believe me because she was such a strong woman."

Mary was eighty-two when she became ill with lung disease and came to live with Yukie and Don. "It was just a joy to have her here with us – to give back, after all the times she had helped me." By that time, Yukie had had all of the joint replacements and was able to take care of Mary. Yukie bathed her, cooked meals, got up in the night as needed and diapered her. "Four years she was with us in our home and I took care of her every day, even though hospice came in for about a year. Anything she needed I did. I prayed that God would give me strength to love Mary and to be with her to the end. And He did!

"Don and I would have to take her to rehab at the hospital and she'd always say, 'Are you going to take me home?'

"Why sure, Mary."

"It isn't that I don't like these people but if I'm going to die, I want to die with people who love me and people I know."

"We'd bring her home and she'd be so happy."

As she began to be in failing health, Mary told Yukie, 'I'm ready to go. Just don't pray to keep me here. Let me go. I don't want to be a burden."

Yukie smiles at the recollection. "How could she ever think of herself as a burden? She blessed my life in so many ways and blessed everyone who knew her."

Yukie remembers, "To see her laying in the bed and wasting away was very hard but nothing could dim her spirit. It was still alive and vivacious. Her friends came by to see her and she was still telling people about Jesus. She lived a full life until the end.

"My life now is very peaceful, very quiet. I love it! I felt that I was here (on this earth) to help others, that was my calling, and I still believe that. I love older people, for the wisdom that they have and the stories. I didn't know if I could ever help people again, but I wanted to and now I am doing it. I don't run around looking for people to help. I just let the Lord bring who He wants to bring. Sometimes these are people I have never met. They will say, 'Someone told me you would pray for cancer.' "

She keeps food in her home to give to people. She and some friends make sure that the people really are in need. "If you sit down and talk with people, you can tell. We give them food, pay for prescriptions, give them Bibles if they don't have Bibles. We don't ask them to pay for our help. We suggest that they do the same thing for someone else when they can. I tell them, 'If it's a single mother in a hamburger place, just pay attention. If there are four of them and she only buys two hamburgers, you can tell they don't have a lot of money and you pay their bill.'"

Yukie also cares for elderly people. She takes them to the doctor, gets their medications, takes them to the grocery store and lets them get what they want. "It's good for them to get out for that short period of time. I let them talk and just listen. One older lady simply likes me to take her out in the car so she can see the mountains. It is a wonderful thing to be able to help others; that's what God wants us to do: touch people, love people.

"But the most important thing I do is pray for people. I've had many, many answers to prayer. The doctors would say, 'We don't understand how your body can heal as quickly as it does, when with rheumatoid arthritis your body is actually fighting itself.' I prayed for healing. But I had no idea how God would do it."

Yukie's knuckles have all been replaced but her hands are still crippled from arthritis. She takes pain medication when she needs it but the pain is nothing like it was. One of her granddaughters is angry that God has not healed her totally, but Yukie claims she *has* been healed. She rejoices that she is able to function; she is able to do what she needs to do.

Yukie prayed for her family. "I believe that all the kids (her siblings) had accepted the Lord when they were about twelve, but I was the first one to re-dedicate my life." She prayed for her brothers and sisters, and especially for her dad to have a close relationship with God. "And my prayers were all answered. I believe that is the greatest inheritance that a child can give a parent or a parent can give a child, is to know that they're in heaven."

Yukie looks forward to seeing Mary in heaven someday. "There was true love between us. I think it's only something God can do, to have a mother-in-law and daughter-in-law love each other as we did."

Yukie Echols (far right), her husband Don, and her mother-in-law, Mary

13

Deacon Lou, Faithful Servant of God – Louis Weitzel

A little boy crouched underneath the bedroom window. He tried not to be seen by his father and the men seated on the front porch. He was all too aware of the guns partly obscured behind the backs of his father's friends, their barrels leaning against the wall of the house. A welcome summer breeze ruffled the curtains and young Lou Weitzel could hear the low murmur of the men chatting quietly, interrupted now and then by the louder voice of a man walking by. "Hello, Urban," the man would call out in a friendly voice. His father would greet the person nonchalantly, saying the neighbor's name.

Lou's heart was beating so hard in his young chest that he thought he might have a heart attack. Many a night he had looked out this very window to see a cross burning in the yard, and heard his father say, "Get away from that window. Do you want to be killed?"

Oh yes, Lou knew what it was like to be a son in the only Catholic family in their small Indiana town during the 1920s. He also knew what it was like to live across the street from the park where every Saturday night the Ku Klux Klan gathered. The men who greeted his father as they passed by to the gathering at the park, were so confident of public acceptance that they distained wearing the traditional white robe and hood of the Klan.

Urban was the prosperous, hardworking part owner and manager of the only lumber yard in town. During these depression years, he and his family made sacrifices so that none of his employees would lose their jobs. Lou had heard his father say, "People will know that we are Christians by the way that we live." Urban Weitzel was not only a devout Catholic, but he had also gained the reputation among many in the town as a man of strong Christian convictions. Lou says, "And I have lived by my father's example all my life; he was my greatest mentor."

Urban also had a sense of humor and when crosses burned in the middle of the night, he would joke, "There's more business for my lumber yard." But young Lou knew on this night there were no jokes. Men from their Catholic Church in a near-by town had come with their guns loaded because his father thought this might be the night when the Klan would burn their house down. The family had received notes slipped under the door threatening to burn them out of the neighborhood before, but Urban had decided that on this night his neighbors needed to know he would use force to defend his home. Lou would always remember that night and the relief his family felt when the threat had passed.

In the town of thirteen hundred Lou estimates that 90% of the population were either members of the Klan or sympathetic to its goals. Through the years, Urban refused to be intimidated. Every Sunday he and his family faithfully got on the Inter-Urban streetcar and traveled seventeen miles to the nearest Catholic Church. "People knew we were different," Lou muses, "but they didn't know why."

As Lou's three older brothers walked home from school, their classmates harassed them, throwing stones and calling them names. However, one father told his four husky sons, close in age to the three brothers, "See that the Weitzel boys get home safely." Viewing the seven young men walking purposefully together, their detractors faded away.

Lou's three brothers left after their sophomore years to enter religious orders; two became priests and one a brother in the Catholic Church. As time passed, Klan leaders were discredited and the organization declined. By the time Lou entered high school his classmates refused to be influenced by their parents' prejudice. Lou was the first Catholic to graduate from the public high school in the small town. He was elected president of his class in his freshman, sophomore, and senior years.

Meanwhile, Urban received permission from the bishop to start a church in his home. Near-by suburbs of Indianapolis were growing rapidly, and the church grew with it. The purchase of a larger house and various additions were needed to accommodate the thriving congregation. In a visit there years later, Lou was gratified to learn that the church now has thirteen hundred families. The church hall is named for Lou's parents: The Urban and Mary Weitzel Hall.

Beginning in his senior year in high school, for three summers, Lou attended President Roosevelt's Citizens Military Training Camps. The war in Europe was beginning to heat up and Lou knew that, as a seasoned military recruit, he was entitled to an officer's commission. However, Lou wanted to fly. "In those days," he recalls, "airplanes were such a novelty that when people heard one, they would run out into the yard, training their eyes on the sky. We all had a fascination with flying."

Lou left his college studies at Notre Dame and Purdue with a determination to train as a pilot and enter the armed forces of the United States. He applied and was accepted for training in the United States Army Air Corps, but after two weeks he was informed *he was not pilot material.* Lou grins as he relates, "They told me I would never learn to fly. So, I wrote the British embassy in Chicago, and they sent me to St. Louis to sign up in the Canadian Air Force and then to Windsor, Ontario for instruction."

Lou was training in Canada when Pearl Harbor was attacked. Factories in the United States went into high gear, manufacturing airplanes in great numbers, but there were few trained pilots. The United States bargained to get American boys back from the Canadian Air Force, settling on $35,000 a head for 800 pilots. Lou says that 99% of those American pilots were men, who like him, had been washed out of training in the U.S. They all enjoyed the fact that the Army Air Corps was now forced to admit the value of their capabilities! Lou was sent back to the United States to locate a crew and a bomber; in three months he was in London flying U.S. combat missions over Germany.

The brief trip home allowed him to propose to Kathleen McCarthy from Detroit whom he had met on a train while he was flying for the Canadians. Quite smitten with this beautiful young lady, Lou visited her family in Detroit. The house was full of young men, friends of Kathleen's brothers, and her father did not realize that a certain airman was there to court his daughter. When Lou sent her an engagement ring, her father demanded. "Who are you engaged to?" When she described Lou, he told her, "I just thought he was one of your brothers' friends!" Lou and Kathleen were married just before he left for England.

Lou tells about an unforgettable experience in 1944. By that time, he was twenty-two, a lieutenant and a veteran B-24 World War

II pilot. In thirty-two missions over Germany, he had never lost a crew member. He thanked God continually that he had overcome the odds, which at that time were 275 to 1 against a bombing crew making it home from all their missions. On this particular day he had no warning that he was destined for a suicide flight into the South of France.

A hand on his shoulder and a quick message spoken into his ear, "You're needed at Headquarters ASAP," mobilized the young airman. Within minutes his long strides took him to the nearby building that was Headquarters. He seated himself quickly, taking note that his crew was in the small audience, along with two other bomber crews.

The orders were short and to the point: General Patton wanted a bridge taken out in advance of his troops in France. As Lou and his co-pilot listened to the weather report, they realized they would not survive this mission. Lou says, "The weather over France was lousy." The bombers would be flying underneath a ceiling of approximately 1000 feet. At 600 – 700 feet the planes had only seconds to get clear of the bombs exploding beneath them. *They would never make it away from their target alive.*

Lou and his crew were trained to obey orders. As they took off, Lou was resigned that this would be his last mission. They flew south to France, and just six minutes from their destination, a voice crackled over the intercom. Patton had been able to take the bridge and would use it to push his tanks into enemy territory. They could return to base. Lou breathed a sigh of relief.

This was only the latest in what had been many close calls for Lou and his crew. As they flew over Germany, they would be locked into formation for eighteen to nineteen minutes until they were able to drop bombs on their target. Unable to go up, down, to the right or left, they were prime targets for the German anti-aircraft guns trained on them from the ground. As his plane honed in to its target, Lou urgently prayed the rosary. Many times his plane was hit, and sometimes he returned to base with just two or three of his four engines. He could recall once at 22,000 feet watching helplessly as a fellow pilot drifted by his window – no parachute. The American had abandoned his disabled plane, frantically using his arms to slow his descent to earth. "These are things you remember," Lou recalls soberly. "You just hope he passed out before he hit the ground."

For his service in Europe and in recognition of his outstanding record in bringing all of his crew members home safely, Lieutenant Louis Weitzel was awarded the Distinguished Flying Cross. Recognizing how fortunate he was to have survived the war, Lou told God: "You brought me out of this, do with me whatever You will."

Having completed the maximum number of missions allowed by the military, Lou was reassigned to the airbase in Brownsville, Texas. Kathleen went into labor with their first child, Tom, on August 14th, 1945, the day the war ended. As she came out of labor, Kathleen could hear the din of car horns, church bells, and people cheering in the streets of Brownsville. With a twinkle in her eye, she told the new father, "I must have done something spectacular."

When time came to leave the Army Air Corps, Lou and Kathleen made the decision to settle in Lou's hometown. Lou's father was still part owner and manager of the lumber yard, and Lou, full of youthful ideas, went to work for his father. However, after almost a year of working together, Lou realized that it was time to move on. It was the age-old problem: his father was content to do things as he always had, and Lou's suggestions for renovating the business caused tension between him and his father. The automobile industry beckoned to Lou with his background in engineering and so he moved his family to Detroit, Michigan.

After two years working for Garwood Corporation, Lou landed a job with Ford Motor Company in Production Control. Computers were just coming into prominence and Lou's boss had confidence that his assistant could learn computer technology. IBM owned all the computers being used by industry, leasing the computer to Ford Motor Company for twenty-four hours a day, seven days a week, at a cost of $150.00 an hour. IBM also controlled who would be trained to operate the computer which occupied a huge room. Lou was sent to downtown Detroit to be tested and scored the highest grade in the class. After two weeks of training, the former pilot found himself with two jobs: computer programmer and trouble shooter. An engineer experienced in computer technology had transferred from General Motors to Ford, and this engineer became Lou's boss.

Because of the cost of operating the computer, it was important that it never be idle. Key punch operators fed data into the machine during the day, and management hoped there would be enough work to keep the computer productive through the night. Whenever there was a problem with the function of the gigantic machine, Ford employees would call Lou at home. "For three years I never got a complete night's sleep," Lou says. Called from deep slumber, Lou would consult computer diagrams spread out in his kitchen so that he could quickly find the problem and advise people on the other end of the phone line. Occasionally, afraid to make a decision about finances, a worker would advise Lou that there was not enough data to keep the computer active. "Should we pay the key punch operator overtime to put more data into the machine?" they would ask.

Exasperated, Lou recalls he would shout, "Don't be stupid! A key punch operator makes $3.25 an hour, and for the computer, whether you use it or not, you pay $150.00 an hour. *Why is this a difficult decision for you to make*!"

"As you can see, I got a reputation," Lou admits with a grin.

"My bosses appreciated that I put in a full day's work. I would tell myself, 'I'm going to be here for the full shift. So, let's do it right. Let's do something worthwhile.'" Lou retired from Ford Motor Company after a distinguished career of thirty-two years.

A year or so after retirement, Lou's wife Kathleen became terminally ill. He nursed her for seven years until her death. As a single widower, Lou remembers saying to himself, "I can spend my time playing golf and sitting on a bar stool, or I can become a deacon and do something fulfilling." Lou chose to enroll in the deaconate program in Lansing, Michigan, finishing in three years. When he sought to enter the priesthood, he was told that at seven-two he was too old. This tickled Lou to mention because at 94, he was one of the oldest actively serving deacons in the United States. His duties included turning on the lights, unlocking and locking doors, setting up for Mass, serving on the altar with the priest, taking the Host to those who are sick and homebound, and giving the Homily once a month. "I didn't do anything that anyone else couldn't do," he says with humility, but he served faithfully wherever he was needed.

Anyone who knows Lou discerns in him a sweet spirit. "When my wife died, I could have been bitter. I did not want to be alone," he admits. "But choosing to become a deacon solved that problem."

Lou is fond of saying he is fortunate to have had four lives: a bomber pilot in World War II, a husband and father, a computer programmer, and a deacon of the Church. He sums up his philosophy of life in this way: "If I did not do everything I could to promote the Christian faith, I would be a failure. Nothing I have done in my lifetime or accomplished was without asking God and receiving grace for it." A legacy Lou would like to pass on to succeeding generations!

At ninety-nine years of age Deacon Lou Weitzel went to his heavenly home on July 15, 2019.

Deacon Lou was the oldest serving Deacon in the United States at the time of his interview.

14

Run to God! – Christiana*

When Christiana* is overwhelmed by her duties as a step mother to three girls, she runs to her clothes closet, shuts the door, and prays. She acknowledges that, had it not been for their Christian faith, she and husband Jake* could have turned to drugs, alcohol, or just talking to friends about their problems. Instead, both of them turned to God for the answers they needed, and without fail, God answered their prayers.

When Christiana and Jake began dating, they both understood that their commitment to each other would have the additional challenge of caring for Jake's daughters, each from a different mother. They saw in the stability of their commitment to each other an opportunity to care for the girls, and if permitted, to support the mothers.

"Let me clarify," Christiana says. "Jake and I are best friends and we love each other deeply. It is very romantic. But we knew that an important priority of our marriage would be the attention we would give to *our three girls*."

When Jake, son of a pastor, graduated high school he rebelled against his church up-bringing. He married his first wife when she became pregnant at fifteen. They divorced after two years of violent arguments. Later, Jake had a daughter each from two other women to whom he was not married. By the time he and Betty met, Jake had turned his life around. One of his primary aims was to responsibly parent his daughters.

Christiana had not grown up in a Christian home although her mother, raised Baptist, always sent her to Vacation Bible School. Her father was a biologist who trained his children to systematically solve problems in a logical manner, but a relationship with God was not a part of his life.

When Betty entered college, she was more interested in partying than in studying. Although she did not last long in college, she met a friend there who was to change her life. The friend invited her to attend a small group Bible study. She was persistent, overcoming Christiana's feelings of inferiority about her lack of biblical knowledge. Finally, Christiana agreed to try it out. Gifted with an outgoing personality, Christiana enjoyed the informality and fun the young adults had together, and in April of 1991 she began to go regularly. She accepted Jesus Christ as Lord of her life and was baptized in December of that year. With renewed purpose, Christiana returned to college and finished her degree. She met and married Jake soon thereafter.

In the first year of their marriage Christiana and Jake were able to focus on their relationship as a couple. Jake's daughters, ages three, eight, and eleven, came every other weekend, but during this first year, the girls lived primarily with their birth mothers.

In June of the second year, a court order brought the middle child, Mary Ann*, to live with them. Mary Ann's mother had been in and out of jail multiple times and most recently had assaulted her ten-year-old daughter. When Mary Ann moved in with Jake and Betty, she struggled against accepting them as her parents. Her mother had warned Mary Ann that Christiana would try to *make* her call her "mother." It would take years before Mary Ann realized that accepting the stability and love Jake and Christiana offered was not a betrayal of her birth mother.

Three months after Mary Ann came to live with them, the oldest daughter, Suzanne*, now thirteen, chose to also live with Jake and Christiana. Suzanne told Christiana she had experimented with sex and alcohol, and knew she would not have a chance for a different life unless she left her mother. Christiana and Jake were glad to have her out of that situation. Fortunately, Suzanne and Mary Ann got along well together. They were less than three years apart, and had had similar life experiences with their birth moms.

The youngest child, Julie*, continued to come every other weekend, and as far as Christiana and Jake knew, everything was stable in her life. Her mother was a single mom, living with her mother, Julie's grandmother. Julie was happy as a lark, a typical youngest child, fitting in with everyone.

The fulltime parenting of Suzanne and Mary Ann was new for Christiana and Jake. Christiana says, "We began to implement what we understood from God's Word. We listened and learned from mentors who gathered around to advise us: grandparents or those whose relationships we wanted to reflect. We may not have known what to do in every situation, but we had an open ear to whatever the kids wanted to tell us. We were excited to have them in our home. *We saw God's hand in all of that.*

"I wouldn't say that the first six months were bliss," Christiana honestly confesses, "but they were challenging in a *good* way and we rose to the occasion. We played with Suzanne and Mary Ann. We encouraged them. We tried to let them know that God wanted something new for their lives; they did not have to look at the shadow of their past. They could start something new for themselves, for their families, for their future."

Jake and Christiana prayed that the girls be set free from the destructive patterns covering many generations, and over their lives in general. They attended sports events and transported their daughters faithfully to practices. They made sure the girls attended church so they could get connected. "*They thrived*," Christiana emphasizes. "They were open to all of it; they just wanted a change."

A year after Suzanne came to live with Jake and Christiana, she began to rebel. Christiana says, "This child was like a bird whose wings had been clipped. Her pattern was to never stay anywhere for any length of time." Suzanne and her mother would occupy an apartment until they could not pay their bills. Then they would move out, leaving all their belongings behind. Now Suzanne indicated to her dad and stepmother that she didn't want to live with them any longer.

The summer after eighth grade Christiana and Jake caught her sneaking out at night to meet a boyfriend. When confronted, she didn't deny it. "I want out," she told them. "I want to go back to Mom's house." Christiana and Jake told her that that was not going to happen, that she had made a decision to live with them and she needed to see it through. Emotionally they wrestled with her all that summer, but when Suzanne started high school in the fall, she began to do better. She was busy playing volleyball and had less time on her hands.

"While I did not pray for this, I thank God that both of these mothers were removed from the situation," Christiana recalls. Suzanne and Mary Ann's birth mothers did not visit or contact their daughters; eventually both mothers were back in jail. Periodically Suzanne and Mary Ann would want to visit their mothers there.

"We were adamant about not letting that happen," Christiana asserts. "We didn't feel that was the way for them to see their mothers. We were very protective of the girls."

When Suzanne turned eighteen in November, she left Christiana and Jake a note telling them what horrible parents they were, and moved in with her boyfriend's parents. Somewhat later she left him and began living with Jake's parents who told Christiana and Jake that they agreed with Suzanne that her parents were too strict. "There were so many levels of hurt but God was there for all of it," Christiana says. The day Suzanne left, the members of Christiana and Jake's small Life Group dropped everything they were doing to come to their home to comfort and care for them. Several of the Pastors from their church visited them in the days that followed and the church prayed for them.

All of the family mourned Suzanne's leaving. Christiana says, "She just tore out my heart and stomped on it. I never felt so much hurt in all my life. When you deal with teenagers, you get caught up in the drama. I was the mother of a teenager and I was in that level of emotion – I was angry. Each of us had to grieve in his own way. With me everything was out in the open, very outward, talking it over with friends. Shortly after Suzanne left, Mary Ann and I cleaned out her closets and I gave all her clothes away. Later, she came to get her clothes, but they were gone."

"Mary Ann was also crushed. She was a freshman in high school and she missed the connection she had with her sister. She had enjoyed talking together about new girlfriends and things happening at school. We talked it through as much as we could," Christiana says. "I called Suzanne on the phone and asked her, 'Why didn't you talk with us about this?'

Suzanne told her, "I had been moving out for two months and you didn't even notice."

"Jake, on the other hand, dealt with it internally; he isolated and struggled with depression. He felt guilty because he had brought these children into my life and contributed to my pain." Christiana tried to console Jake that he could not protect her from the trials of life.

For his part, Jake encouraged Christiana, saying, "You're the mother they should have had, the mother they always wanted."

"Luckily, even in our woundedness, we turned to God," Christiana says. "I was in a *Moms in Touch* prayer group. I got a lot of support and encouragement from them." Books by Stormi Omartian were also helpful: *The Power of a Praying Parent*, and *Praying for your Adult Children. I Lay My Isaac Down* by Carol Kent helped Christiana commit Suzanne to God and trust Him to care for her. Christiana shared what she was learning with Jake who was not a reader. His main source of comfort came from being in worship at their church and prayer times with the Lord. Having people pray for him also gave Jake strength and encouragement. "Our heavenly Father held us and grew us through those times," Christiana says.

"We were connected to other blended families, but everyone's story is different. There were many times when we felt isolated, that nobody could fully understand what we were going through. We can look back now and see how that was the subtle hand of the enemy, Satan, because that's how he wants the family to feel: broken down, isolated, with no one to support you."

Later that next spring Suzanne asked to meet with her parents. She let them know she was pregnant. She now wanted them to be a part of her life and the child's life.

Christiana told her, "Listen, I am going to need some time. I had the privilege of being your mother and you rejected me. Obviously, I forgive you, but I'm going to need some time to trust we can have a relationship." Christiana says, "It was a bit rocky for a while."

When Suzanne's baby was born, Christiana and Jake went to the hospital, brought gifts for the baby, and did their best to express support to the new mom, but Suzanne seemed distant. So, they were not surprised that she turned mainly to her latest boyfriend's parents to babysit.

That fall when Suzanne's baby turned one year old, Julie's grandmother called to say that her daughter, Julie's mother, had been arrested for drug use. Jake and Christiana now learned that Julie had kept her mother's drug problems hidden from them for two or three years. Although the grandmother asked that Christiana and Jake not pursue custody of Julie, they did, and were thrilled when it was granted. Christiana says, 'We did not want any of the kids to ever say there was a time when their dad did not fight for them.'"

In a weak moment Christiana was talking to God with her customary honesty: "I thought I was done," she told Him. "I'm tired of mothering other people's children with all their issues." The Lord gave her a moment of clarity. She felt God's love and His presence. She had this thought: *"The youngest will be the redemption of the other two."*

When Julie came, Mary Ann, the middle daughter, began to rebel. She resented sharing her parents' attention. Both girls were seeing counselors and Mary Ann was dealing with some issues of abuse with a prayer and healing team at church. Christiana says, "There was definitely spiritual warfare going on. She would come at us physically and we would have to restrain her. She was also verbally abusive. It was a difficult time for me. Just when I was despairing of my bond with her, she would do something that revealed her desire to have a close connection." She began to call Christiana "Mom."

"Mary Ann always wanted to be the perfect child with me; she saw how Suzanne's leaving had hurt, and she never wanted to hurt me like that. On her eighteenth birthday she crawled into bed with me, and said, 'I'm still here.' "

Suzanne had been out of touch with her parents for several years, when one day Jake got a Facebook message from a gentleman named Roy*. He told Jake, "I am Suzanne's husband and I want you to know Suzanne misses you *so much.* We're in the hospital getting ready to have our baby. We want you to be a part of our lives and our children's lives. Here's where we are—if you can bring yourselves to come and see us."

Christiana was skeptical, but of course, wild horses couldn't have kept Jake away. She told him to go to the hospital and she was going out with some of her girlfriends. "Call and tell me if this isn't a set-up," she told Jake. "With all we've been through, I'm not buying it." Jake went to the hospital and there was instant forgiveness. Christiana says, "As the Bible says, 'And I will restore to you the years the locust hath eaten.' (Joel 2:25 - KJV)

Tears were shed. Suzanne's first child said, "Do you remember me?"

"So precious! We have not looked back since."

Suzanne made a commitment to them, "I will never let anything come between us. Never!"

Christiana recalls that moment, "It was God's forgiveness at its finest. We thought it would take years to repair that relationship. I would say to anyone, if there are any family relationships in your life that are broken and you think it is going to take twenty, thirty, or forty years to be repaired, God can fix that in an instant. For us, it was just His timing. I can't explain it." Christiana loves her two grandchildren and she and Jake spend lots of time with them.

The summer after Mary Ann graduated from high school her parents were happy with whom she was dating and gave her more freedom. She moved into a college dorm so she could take pre-freshman classes. She did not handle her new freedom well. At one point she was arrested by police for public intoxication. She came home after that summer and told her parents, "I can't go back. I know I'll continue in that lifestyle. Don't make me go back."

Christiana and Jake warned her, "We still have a younger child so if you're going to live with us, it's still house rules. Julie needs to get her sleep for school. You will have a curfew and you need to work fulltime to pay off college loans." Mary Ann lasted two weeks before she moved out.

She began hanging out at the University campus with a group of friends who frequented a Middle Eastern drug smoking paraphernalia shop. There she met the nephew of the owner who was Jordanian. He needed a green card in order to stay in the United States and so they agreed to marry. His part of the bargain was to give her a place to live and to support her financially so she would be free to do whatever she wanted. In the same town as the University were many of Christiana's extended family. They were looking out for Mary Ann, asking her, "Hey, what are you doing? I really encourage you to move back home with your parents, get a job, pursue your education." Mary Ann went ahead with the marriage and it was not until a month later that she told her parents.

A year into the marriage Mary Ann let her parents know her husband was abusing her. She told Christiana and Jake that her husband would take off in the middle of the night and drive to Texas. Although Mary Ann did not know anything about what he was doing, a friend of Jake and Christiana's told them Mary Ann's husband's family was involved in drug runs. "Oh yes," the police told them, "We have him in our sights." Jake and Christiana were concerned about Mary Ann's safety. They begged her to leave him.

Christiana says, "If our youngest (Julie) were to be abducted, she would never be able to get away. But Mary Ann has such an attitude that they would stop the car at the end of the street and kick her out." She smiles, "Mary Ann will test you and fight with you to the nth degree." The summer of that year Mary Ann's husband granted her a divorce. At the time of this interview, she is back with the boyfriend of whom her parents approve. They are not married, but are living together and he loves her very much. Christiana says, "As a mother, you would love for them to marry, but I am not pushing them. Taking into consideration the path Mary Ann was on in the beginning, I am grateful for where she is. We try to reinforce their relationship and their love for each other. We are thankful to have their ears."

"When the middle child moved out," Christiana says, "the youngest became the child I never thought she could be. Julie was an introvert, a wallflower in the shade of her two older sisters. Now, my baby girl began to blossom. She led us in learning about her personality and she even learned a lot about herself. When one of her sisters comes to visit about the time Julie arrives home from school, Julie lets them know that this is her time to talk with us about her day. Her attitude says, 'This is *my time.*' This child has loved me in more ways as a parent than I could imagine."

Christiana looks back on blessings that have come from being willing to embrace parenting the three girls. "We are still growing. I had this view that once the girls graduated high school and were on their own, that our relationship would suddenly change. We would have more fun and I would counsel them, but be less involved in their lives. Instead, I think they need me as much, or perhaps even more, than before. That's been a big learning curve for me that I didn't expect. I have learned that when they are facing decisions, be it about a job, a relationship, or going back to give their birth moms another chance, I will say, 'I'm going to be praying about that.' Or I might say, 'This is your decision.' The relationships with their moms are a dilemma we have seen them struggle with all of their lives. They want

Mom to be different but their moms have gone on in their cycles. We pray for them too, to be a friend to the girls. We have had many wonderful moments with our kids that we wish their moms could have had. We're the fortunate ones."

She says, "The biggest thing I learned through these experiences is how God parents me. I was a type A child, and I suspect I will be a recovering perfectionist the rest of my life. I wanted things to go a certain way when the girls came to live with us. I was resolved that we were going to grow, and the girls were going to understand what had happened. They were never going to go back to what was. After Suzanne left, it crushed my heart. Then, I began the learning process of understanding how God parents me. If God parents me with the freedom to love Him even in the worst situation, why can't I give my children that same freedom? It really changed my perception of how God's love works."

Jake and Christiana mentor couples in their church. Christiana says, "We feel strongly about investing in other couples, using what God has taught us. We ask specifically for second marriages involving the blending of couples where children are involved. We are not trying to change outcomes, but just to let them know they are not alone. We've been through it."

"My husband and I are very open in saying that we love God more than we love each other. There is no way we can grow closer together unless we keep God at the center of our relationship."

"My advice to anyone struggling with difficult situations would be this," Christiana says: "*Don't let go of God.* In the worst moments when you feel tempted to run to whatever it is: another man, alcohol or drugs, to a friend just to chat about the situation—just run to God. ***Just run to God.***"

* Real names are not used.

15

Faith That Triumphs – Linda M. Zarate Stephens

Isaiah the Prophet stood beside the sick bed of Hezekiah, King of Israel (2 Kings 20: 1b), "This what the Lord says: Put your house in order, because you are going to die; you will not recover." And as Hezekiah wept, Isaiah left the palace.

Linda Stephens looked up in shock from the Gideon Bible she was holding. That morning in 1998 she noticed the nurses glancing in her direction and whispering. Linda suspected the news from the results of her ultrasound were bad. So, the vivacious Hispanic mother of two picked up the Bible asking, "God, show me what *You* say is happening. I will only stand on Your word." Then at random she confidently opened the Bible and read: *"Put your house in order because you are going to die."*

A couple of weeks prior, Linda had visited her primary care physician for a vitamin B shot to help with anemia. Her doctor noticed her abdomen was extended, and Linda admitted that when she pressed there, a pain shot from her abdomen to her back. Her doctor insisted Linda have an ultrasound. Today the petite forty-seven-year-old would get the news.

"Ohh Lord, you don't beat around the bush, do you?" Linda was familiar with the Bible passage in 2 Kings, and her next thought was, "Calm down and read the rest of the story."

Again, she looked at the open Bible in her hands and read, "(2 Kings 20:2-3) "Hezekiah turned his face to the wall and prayed to the Lord, 'Remember now, O Lord, how I have walked before you faithfully and with wholehearted devotion and have done what is good in your eyes.' And Hezekiah wept bitterly.

"Before Isaiah had left the middle court, the word of the Lord came to him: 'Go back and tell Hezekiah, the leader of my people, This is what the Lord, the God of your father David, says: I have heard your prayer and seen your tears; I will heal you. On the third day from now you will go up to the temple of the Lord. I'm going to add fifteen years to your life.' " (2 Kings: 20: 4-5a)

Linda thought, "Okay, God. If You're giving me fifteen more years, I can handle that. I will stand on Your Word, regardless of what the doctors say." Linda thought of her oldest son with spinal bifida. He was dating someone and they were planning to marry. She wanted to see *both* of her sons marry and to see grandchildren, and Linda wanted to be the partner her husband needed. Yes, fifteen years would be a precious gift.

By this time, Linda was called into the doctor's office and her friend, Diane, an oncology nurse, joined them. The doctor's mouth was tight and his eyes sober as he turned in her direction. Linda looked at her friend, Diane, and the compassion on her face told Linda she had been right: *the news was not good.*

"We've looked at your charts; we've looked at the ultra-sound, and we're going to send you for another CAT scan. We have to do a biopsy but from the looks of things you've got Lymphoma."

Linda looked uncomprehendingly at the doctor, "Maybe it's just a benign tumor."

"No, you have Lymphoma. Now we just have to figure out what kind."

In shock, Linda could hardly breathe, her mind refused to grasp the truth of the diagnosis. She stared blankly as the doctor continued speaking, but nothing he said registered. Her heart felt heavy with the thought, "Oh my God, *Lymphoma*. I have received a death sentence. It's cancer by another name!" She couldn't believe this was happening to her. Even though she had moments before read the Scripture that prophesied a life-threatening illness, the reality sent her heart racing. Her hands were clammy, and she felt faint and sick to her stomach. She reminded herself that God had been faithful to her through many trials in the past. *She would surely need Him now.*

Linda was raised in a "Christian" family, her mom more spiritual than her dad. Her maternal grandfather was a Baptist minister who was saved when he was forty years old. He began the first Hispanic Protestant church in Lenawee County, an area of Michigan where a sizeable population of former migrant workers from Mexico had settled. Linda's grandfather often went into Mexico and Guatemala to preach and evangelize, and faith was an integral part of Linda's family.

At age twelve as Linda listened to an evangelist from Guatemala, the Lord spoke to her heart. She felt the weight of her sin, her need of God, and she went to the altar to give her heart to Jesus. She recalls, "I was sincere, but at that time there was nothing in place to disciple me or to encourage me to study the Bible. At twelve years of age, I don't think the adults took me seriously – you're still a kid.

But that is a very crucial time: you are starting to notice the world; you are starting to notice boys; you're beginning to be aware of a lot of things."

While Linda grew up knowing her grandfather's story and admiring his faithfulness to Jesus Christ, her youthful spirit felt constricted by his old-fashioned rules: women couldn't wear pants, jewelry, or makeup, and men and women couldn't swim together. Linda says, "I rebelled and I went the other way! I have always loved jewelry, fashion, and makeup. The pull of the world and all of these shiny things drew me away from the church in high school. I had friends who were not Christians, who influenced my choices and drew me into doing things I should not have done."

At age eighteen, Linda left home to live in a hippy commune. "I got into drugs: LSD, marijuana, and a lot of peripheries. I became sexually active. At first it was exciting, but I also found it dissatisfying. At that time there was talk about expanding your mind, your consciousness. People were experimenting with spiritualism. They were trying to connect with their spirit because they recognized there had to be something more than this material world. This was the time of the Civil Rights Movement and the War in Viet Nam. I was in the middle of all of that, and being young, I could not understand it. The atrocities we were seeing on television, all of it was *just so heavy* and weighed on my spirit! I think my generation got "high" to forget. We wanted to be joyful in the moment, to live life fully. That works for a while, but then you ask yourself, 'What am I here for? Why am I here? What is my purpose?' I had all these questions!

"Of course, my friends and I would get into discussions about God, and I felt the Holy Spirit drawing me. The Word says, 'No man can come to Me, except the Father... draw him.' (John 6:44 KJV) The Lord never stopped drawing me. I was His. I had committed myself to Him at age twelve. Even though I strayed, like the Prodigal

Son in the Bible, He never stopped waiting for me to come home." (Luke 15:11 – 32)

One night, Linda and a friend were crashing on mattresses in an apartment, high on marijuana. Linda passed out, her long hair spread out on the mattress and onto the floor. There was a candle burning on the floor, in a plastic candleholder. As the candle burned down, the floor caught fire. Both girls narrowly escaped, and Linda was shocked at how close they had come to death. "What would have happened to me? What happens when I die? Is there a heaven? And where would I go?" she thought.

The next evening Linda and a group of friends were in the home of a Hispanic friend, getting ready to go out and party. There were also some African-American friends in the group. The girl's father came home unexpectedly and was incensed that his daughter was with African-Americans and also that they were leaving to party. Her father came after them with his belt, flinging the buckle in every direction and spouting vulgarities. Linda says, "Everyone scattered like cockroaches. It wounded my spirit, and I thought, 'Why do Hispanics hate African-Americans so? Why do they hate me? This is such a crazy world. How can this be?' "

She started walking home, weeping as she went, her heavy eye makeup accentuating her tear-streaked face. People looked at her strangely. Once again, she felt the weight of condemnation. Questions were running through her mind. "How can I bring change to this world? I've tried church, and it isn't real, it doesn't work." Then unbidden came this strong impression to her mind:

"Wait. Back up just a bit here and think. All the things that you've been doing, have they satisfied you so far? Are you satisfied with your life, the way that it's going? Is this how you want to be when you're fifty or sixty years of age?"

Linda was taken aback, "Ah, what?"

"Are you so satisfied with the way your life is going now, that you wouldn't try something new?"

"I would...I would try something new because this isn't working."

"What you term love is not love at all. It's just sex – any dog can have sex."

Linda was shocked. These were not her thoughts. It had to be the voice of God speaking to her. The internal Voice continued, *"And as far as philosophizing with your friends when you are high, what has it changed? Has it changed you?"*

"I had to face these truths. No, it hadn't changed me. It had *diminished* me. Sleeping with this one and that one and still not feeling loved made me feel less than. As I felt the weight of that truth and my sin, I couldn't bear it. I was crying hysterically and *no one* stopped to ask me why, or if I was okay. I wondered if there was any hope for me at all. I felt like a discarded dirty rag that had no purpose or use."

When she got home, Linda went to her room but she couldn't seem to stop crying. She thought, "What's going to happen to me? What purpose does my life have? How am I going to change?" She began to cry out to God, "God, if you're there, if you can hear me, heal me! Cleanse me! Help me! Save me from myself."

She had been crying for about three hours and finally was all cried out. She started to leave her room but there on the corner of her desk lay a tiny Bible. Her ten-year old sister, Sylvia, had heard her crying and had placed it there; it was the only thing Sylvia could think of that might help her sister.

Linda picked up the small Bible and looked up at the ceiling, "God, if you're really there, and you're hearing me, I need to know three things: *One*, if I decide to be a Christian, I need to know that I'm not going to be alone in this, that you're going to be with me. *Two*, I need to know that I will find the peace that I have been looking for and not finding in drugs or sex or in any of the philosophies of this world. *Three*, I don't want to be afraid of dying and not knowing where I'm going. If you can answer these three things, I will follow you all the days of my life."

Linda opened the little Bible and it fell open to Judges chapter 6:23 (KJV) where God is speaking to Gideon: "Peace be unto thee. Surely, I will be with thee. Fear not, thou shalt not die."

Linda was astounded! "Oh my God, you *are* real. You heard me. How did you do this? You put this in my room; you knew that I would need it. You love me, and you hear me." She started to cry in joy and lifted her hands, "Thank you, God. Thank you, Jesus." At that moment she felt the presence of God come upon her and cleanse her of every sin. He was making her brand new. She couldn't deny what was happening. She went out into the living room where her sister was watching her.

"What's wrong with you?" Sylvia knew Linda did drugs and she was terrified.

"Nothing's wrong with me now. Jesus just saved me. And God is real!"

Overcome with relief, Sylvia began to cry.

Linda says, "I fell in love with Jesus that day and I still love Him dearly. He's been the center of my life. Everything I have done has been with Him in the forefront, and I want to keep it that way until the day I die. The love of God the Father became real in my life too. And that is the most precious thing, to know that kind of love from a father, because I didn't have that from my natural father."

After she graduated from high school, Linda went to a Christian Bible college in rural Ohio, a place recommended by her grandfather. She loved studying the Bible and began to find answers for many of her questions. However, Linda was conscious that she did not fit in, not only because she was Hispanic but the lifestyle at the college was very conservative: skirts had to be worn down to your ankles, no jewelry, no makeup. Linda made accommodations by wearing skirts to the top of her knees and only a little makeup, some mascara, quite a change from her previous hippy garb of miniskirts. Nevertheless, she got demerits for these things and one day the dean of women called her out in front of everyone in the cafeteria. The administration told Linda they were going to send a letter home to her parents. Linda sensed God was telling her it was time to return to her hometown of Adrian. She had a burden for young people in the hippy community who had the same questions she had had. After her training in Bible College, Linda was confident she could help them find answers.

Linda's mother allowed her and a few Catholic girlfriends from high school to clean out the back of their house which had been a TV repair shop. Linda told her young friends what had happened in her life. They, too, believed everybody needed God. They helped her clean up the room and paint, and a Christian businessman gave them random couch cushions and carpet squares. They called their church "The Way" because that was the name given churches in the New Testament. They were also referring to the Bible verse, "Jesus said, 'I am the way and the truth and the life. No one comes to the Father except through me.' " (John 14:6)

"We would meet to talk and play the guitar, sing and make up songs, and study the Bible. It was a wonderful time. On the west coast a revival called the Jesus Movement was also stirring young people. I felt God working, not just with our group but worldwide. The heart cry of my generation was to know Jesus."

The first night that The Way opened there was a drug bust in Adrian, and twenty-one kids were arrested and their names published in the newspaper. At The Way, they took the newspaper and prayed over every name. One of those busted had in his pocket a tract that Linda had been distributing all over town. It read: LSD:

Lord, Savior, Deliverer! The police saw the letters LSD and thought they had some evidence, but when they saw it was a tract, they crumbled it up and threw it away. The young man, from whom they had taken the tract, picked it out of the trash and put it back in his pocket. That night God began to deal with him. When he left jail, he sought Linda at The Way to learn more about Jesus.

When two of the men got out of jail, they didn't have a place to stay. Linda's mom "adopted them" and took them into her home for several months, until they could get on their feet and find jobs. Linda says, "They are like my brothers." The Way lasted about three years, until the young people were in their twenties and married. Linda observes with anticipation, "When we do get to heaven, we're going to have so much to rejoice about. It's going to take us all of eternity to tell our stories.

"In every dark place, He has never failed me, He has never left me. Our trials are not just about us. God sends us to be witnesses – He tells us to let our light shine before men that they may see our good works and glorify our Father who is in heaven. (Matthew 5:14 KJV) Light is not appreciated unless it is dark. Even a little candle can light a dark room. So, God sent me to some dark places." It was not long before Linda's faith in God would be tested.

Linda was in her early twenties when she had her first child. She thought the kicks she was feeling were his feet, but they were not. Her baby was paralyzed from the waist down. When he was born, his upper body had a lot of strength. His arms were well developed, but his legs had formed upward and his feet looked like praying hands; they were clubbed. He had a hole in his spine about the size of a fifty-cent piece, but it had a thin layer of skin over that. There was a deformation at the back of his skull where the spinal fluid from the brain had accumulated. He was hydrocephalic and had spinal bifida.

As Linda lay on the table following the delivery, she began to pray, "God, I don't understand. What I know is that you spoke to me and told me that his name was to be Judah, which means *praise*, and Elijah, which means *called of God*. Now, although it looks bad, I know there is a purpose even in this, and I trust you implicitly, Father." With her surrender came peace. Linda prayed many prayers over Judah in the intervening years and watched him thrive, becoming a man called of God, productive, bringing praise to the Lord.

Now, here she was again in a dark place, with a cancer diagnosis. Linda clung to the Word of God with daily readings and devotionals. Each day she looked for an encouraging word and would write that word down in her journals. Early in her treatments God's Voice spoke within her spirit saying, "I'm going to heal you and give you a testimony." Linda chose to trust that promise, even though the second CT scan and biopsy revealed she had Non-Hodgkin's Lymphoma. The tumor was large, 21 ½ centimeters; she looked pregnant.

She looked online at Lymphoma and was terrified. She learned that Non-Hodgkins Lymphoma is the hardest cancer to bring into remission because it is in your lymph nodes, in your blood, and it can be in your bones. Later she also learned that she was stage four which meant that some of her organs were also compromised. Her spleen was enlarged and sticking out from beneath her ribcage. Linda wept. "God help me with this."

God spoke to her spirit and said, "Do you remember the story of David and Goliath? Instead of looking at the size of your giant, look at the size of your God."

Linda's diagnosis came in the fall of 1998 but she waited until after Christmas to begin treatment. She didn't know what to expect and she wanted her family to enjoy their holiday. Her children did not grasp that Linda was gravely ill. They had never seen her weak or sick so they were in denial. She could see they thought, "Mom's always strong; she's got a lot of faith. God's got this."

Meanwhile, Linda, herself, was wrestling with all kinds of emotions. "You think about all those things you will miss, but then in my Spirit God kept telling me, 'I'm going to heal you and give you a testimony.' I could always stand upon His Word, but my body was telling me differently. My body was weak and I was out of breath."

On Dec. 27th Linda started a combination of chemo drugs called "The Chop Treatment." Each of the drugs was targeted to break the tumor into pieces. In the process it killed new growth in all the cells of her body, including hair. Linda says, "I looked like a dog with mange. Because I am Hispanic, I started looking sallow, my complexion turned yellow. Not a pretty sight." After the first week of chemo, she was in the shower and hair started to come out in handfuls. She decided to go to the salon and have all her hair shaved off and purchase a wig. Her mom and her sister came with her to the beauty parlor.

Linda told the operator, "Give me a G.I. Jane." She expected her sister to be emotional because, Linda says laughing, "She is a drama queen," but even her mom began to bawl. When the beautician turned Linda around to see the results in the mirror, Linda couldn't stop laughing. Her head was *so* round! She tried on various wigs but they were heavy, and scratchy. After a few months of tolerating the wigs, she switched to bandanas, but then her mom made Linda little knitted caps in various colors.

Linda was scheduled to have a treatment every three weeks for a year. At her second treatment her doctor told her, "Mrs. Stephens, we have some bad news and some worse news."

"Hit me with the worst news first."

"Well, you might have two types of cancer. The tumor in the abdomen has developed into a different kind of Lymphoma and is resistant to the chemotherapy. Secondly, you are bleeding internally and we don't know where it's coming from. We are going to give you blood transfusions as you need them, probably every three weeks."

"Okay, God, this is what they said. What does your Word tell me?" And that is when the Holy Spirit again gave Linda the Scripture about King Hezekiah, this time in Isaiah 38:1-5, and the promise that God was giving her fifteen more years. 'Okay, Lord, I'll fight some more. If you will walk with me through this, we'll take it one day at a time.'"

After six weeks, when they saw that the chemo was still not working, they added the Adriamycin, which is called the "fire drug". It's bright orange and if it drops on the patient's skin, it burns all the way to the bone. Linda remembered before her diagnosis reading the Scripture in Isaiah 43:2b: "When you walk through the fire, you will not be burned; the flames will not set you ablaze." She had been told about the fire drug from her nursing friend, Diane, and was confident that God would be with her should she have that drug. Now that she was facing the actual treatment, Linda was frightened. The nurse suited up in two gowns, several pairs of gloves, and a covering for the hair. She approached Linda carrying a large needle.

"What are you doing?"

"Oh, this is just protocol for the drug."

Linda learned that the IV has to be moved around, given in different veins, because it scars the vein wherever it enters the body and makes the vein sore. She watched the orange medicine coming down the clear tubing and as it drew nearer to entering her body, she looked over at her husband and her brother and said, "*Pray! I'm so terrified*!" She felt like criminals must feel when they are being fed a lethal injection. It started stinging as it entered the vein.

"Nurse, nurse, is it supposed to sting?"

"Honey, if it was outside the vein, you would know because it would really burn."

"That's not any comfort." Linda closed her eyes and began to pray. She felt someone hold her hand – she thought it was the nurse, but when she opened her eyes, there was no one there. "Thank you, Lord," she breathed, and at that moment she was bathed in peace.

"There were five or six hospital stays, and trips to the emergency room in between, because my immune system was so low that I would catch everything." She had days of discouragement when she had pity parties and would cry because she was so weak and sick. In the past she had everything on her calendar, so many things to get done in a day. "When you have cancer, everything is on hold except fighting for your life, every day battling fears. Every day was such a lesson, because I didn't have a choice but to sit still; I had no energy.

"Through every fear, every tormenting jab of the enemy, I had to face it and fight. I knew God had a purpose and I didn't think of giving up, at least not then. As time went on, I was able to be at both of my sons' weddings. God gave Judah a wonderful Christian wife. I cried through the whole ceremony, 'God, you are so faithful and good. You gave Judah just what he wanted and you let me see it.' I was also able to see my first grandson born, to have him hold my finger with his little hand."

During that year of chemo, Linda's white blood cells were killed, so she took drugs to help create both red and white blood cells. The drug to create white blood cells was exceedingly painful because it forced the bone marrow to create the needed cells. She would get back aches and, as the drug worked in her larger bones, the pain came over her in excruciating waves. She struggled to sleep at night. She was neutropenic, which means she had no immunity. She had to be careful not to be around people who were sick.

Nausea was an ever-present struggle. She had no desire to eat and, because she wasn't able to eat, her hypoglycemia kicked in and she had migraines which caused vomiting. The doctors had given her medicine to check for internal bleeding and that medicine was making her loopy.

Her sister told her later, "Linda, in the midst of all of that, you were loopy as anything but you asked the nurse if she had ever heard from God, if she knew your Jesus? If she knew there was a God? I could not believe that even as you're sitting there in pain, going through your ordeal, you're talking to people about the love of God." She had been saying to Linda, "Why would God give you cancer? Out of all of us, you've been serving Him ever since you were eighteen years old."

Linda answered her, "God didn't give me cancer. It runs in our family. It's something we have to go through. But God has a purpose and a plan, you wait and see."

"The cancer did not stop me from going to church or from doing what I wanted to do. I loved to sing so when I felt strong enough, I would go to church and sing as part of the praise and worship team. I would think, 'If this is my last day on earth, what do I want to be found doing –that which I love. I love to worship; I love to pray; I love to talk about the Lord.' And everywhere I went I tried to share my faith with someone. I was believing God for miracles but *one day at a time*." Linda gained strength from being able to encourage others.

Everyday God would give her a fresh word. Some days she was so weak that all she could do was stay in bed and sleep, but Linda says, "The Word never fails. It is a Living Word." When she was afraid, she would quote 2 Timothy 1:7 NKJV "For God has not given us a spirit of fear but of power, of love, and of a sound mind." Linda says, "Just like the example of when the devil was tempting the Lord Jesus in the wilderness in Matthew chapter 4 verse 3, The devil said, 'Boy, you really are hungry. You might want to change these stones into bread, if you really are the Son of God.' And Jesus would quote him a Scripture: 'It is written, man shall not live by bread alone but by every word that proceeds out of the mouth of God, verse 4 NASB.' And that was spiritual food to Jesus. That same spiritual food kept me going.

"The first time I went to the hospital, of course I complained: 'This is so inconvenient. I don't want to be here. This is so uncomfortable. I can't sleep at night. Why are you waking me up in the middle of the night to weigh me, to take my blood work or to take a urine sample?' It didn't make sense to me. But they were trying to save my life; I realized how ungracious and ungrateful I was being. They were trying to help me but I was becoming annoyed.

As Linda recalled Romans 8:28 (NKJV), "And we know that all things work together for good to those who love God, to those who are called according to His purpose," she realized God had a purpose in putting her where she was.

"Alright God, what do you want from me? What do you want my response to be?" Linda began to look at it from that point of view.

The Holy Spirit quickened to her (Matthew 5:16 KJV), telling her that He had called her to "let your light shine before men, that they may see your good works and glorify your Father which is in heaven." Linda understood she was to let her light shine, even in her worst moments, just like the disciples.

In 1999 she got the news for the second time that the tumor was still growing and that remission was only partial. She had to choose between two treatments: one experimental called Bexxar, or a bone marrow transplant. "Lord, I thought you told me you were going to heal me. Here we go again!"

She didn't want to have a bone marrow transplant because she knew it was an ordeal, and she was already so tired from regular blood transfusions. Also, she learned that with a transplant you have to take non-rejection drugs all your life, because you have someone else's bone marrow. So, Linda chose Bexxar. She learned it's an immune-therapy with a radioactive isotope attached, that would target and dissipate the tumor.

Once she and her doctors decided she should have Bexxar, other difficulties arose. Her husband's insurance did not want to pay for it. She had to be her own advocate with the insurance company. She thought to herself, "As if I needed this, the extra stress!"

Her doctor in Ann Arbor was writing the insurance company, and in his letter, Linda read, "Would you rather pay $150,000 to $250,000 for the bone marrow transplant or $5000 for Bexxar?" He wrote that every lymph node and her spleen were involved, a seriousness of prognosis that Linda learned for the first time.

She prayed, "Lord, I would rather do the Brexxar treatment; I can't fight any more. I'm so tired, God, just so tired. I don't know how much more I can take of this, but if I have to go through something else, I would choose this. So, somehow in the heavenlies could you loose the funding for the Bexxar because my insurance doesn't want to pay it?"

Three days later a friend knocked on Linda's door. She said, "Sister Linda, I've been praying for you."

Linda said, "Thank you, I appreciate that."

"I have come to bless you. Would you let me bless you?"

"Okay. Won't you come in?"

"While I was praying for you, God told me to write you a check." She handed Linda a check for $5000 and said, "Don't ever say my name because I want God to get the glory for this." Linda showed her the letter the doctor had written in which was the amount needed for the Bexxar treatment, $5000. The woman began to cry. "I knew I heard from God, I *knew* it!"

"Let's thank God together because I know from here on out, God is going to do great things."

When Linda went in for the dosimetry dose of Bexxar in January 2000, her doctor was looking at her chart and scratching his head. "Mrs. Stephens, weren't you getting transfusions every three weeks for the past year?" She told him she was. He then asked her when was her last transfusion and when she said it was November of 1999, he said "Are you sure?"

"Yes, I am sure. I would remember because it is a three-hour ordeal. Is there something I should be worried about?"

"No, for the first time since I began treating you, your blood work is normal. What happened?"

Linda smiled at him and said, "All I can say, doctor, is that two months ago I went forward in my church, and they laid hands on me and prayed. Since that time, God must have done a miracle. Doctor, God is going to do great things for me. Just you wait and see."

With Bexxar there was just one treatment. Linda was radioactive for the first two to three days so she slept upstairs by herself. To protect her family from the radioactivity, she had to wipe down the toilette with alcohol every time she used it and keep a distance of three to four feet from other people. Miraculously, Linda had no nausea or side effects.

Three months after the Bexxar treatment, Linda went to the Fitness Center. She had been weak for so long that her muscles had atrophied. She had no strength and no energy, but she was determined to work to get her strength back.

When she went back for her first CAT Scan three months later, her color was back, she had gained a little bit of weight, and her hair was starting to come back in curly. When the doctor came in to give her the results, he said, "Mrs. Stephens, you look wonderful! What have you been doing?" She told him that she had joined the Ladies Gym to get her strength back, and he was horrified. He scolded her, reminding her that her immune system was compromised and she was vulnerable. When she asked the doctor what was in the report, he shrugged, "Whatever you're doing, keep doing it because the tumor is now just a shadow and it is starting to deteriorate.

"I told you, Doctor, that God is going to do great things for me!"

She had to go back every three months for the next two years and then it was every six months for the next year. Her original diagnosis was in 1998, and now she has been in remission twenty-three years. Linda's original prognosis was that she had six months to a year to live, but they hadn't told her that until later. Linda says, "God in his mercy kept some of that information from me so I would continue to fight. Sometimes I think we give up too soon, too easily."

After seven years of remission, her doctor told her enthusiastically, "Everything we thought was going to happen to you didn't happen." At that point, Alex Barrinston interviewed Linda for the New York Times. The article was an exposé that doctors were not allowing people to be referred out of their jurisdiction because of the money that could be made. Out of the three people interviewed, Linda was the longest survivor. http://www.nytimes.com/2007/07/14/health/14lymphoma.html God had promised to give Linda a testimony, and so he had, "...exceedingly abundantly, above all she could ask or think... ." (Ephesians 3:20 KJV)

"There are good things that happen. People have different degrees of faith but God honors them all." Linda quotes Jesus in Matthew 17:20 (RSV) "...if you have faith as a grain of mustard seed, you will say to this mountain, 'Move from here to there,' and it will move; and nothing will be impossible to you.'"

Linda has asked the Lord that at the end of her life she would be more fruitful than at the beginning, and that she would bring Him glory. She says that every year she grows stronger as does her trust in God. Each year at the anniversary of her diagnosis Linda shares her picture on Facebook: bald headed and between two pillars with the title "*Samsonette*." Like Samson of the Old Testament, who through the power of God pulled down the pillars of the heathen temple, Linda tells again of God's faithfulness. She recalls how the Lord answered her prayers and miraculously healed her of stage IV Non-Hodgkins Lymphoma.

Psalm 92:15 in the Amplified Bible says, "(They are living memorials) to show that the Lord is upright and faithful to His promises; He is my rock and there is no unrighteousness in Him."

"Samsonette" Linda Zarate Stephens during her battle with fourth stage Lymphoma claimed the power of God would heal her and give her a testimony. And He did.

Invitation

Dear Reader,

I hope you have been inspired and uplifted by the stories in this book. Each of the storytellers has shared with you that Jesus is their "living hope", giving them strength, healing, and deliverance in the everyday struggles of life. If you have never given your life into His hands, I invite you to do so today. Just pray a simple prayer that can be something like this: "Father God, I know You love me, and that the Lord Jesus gave His life to take away my sins. Lord Jesus, please come into my heart and help me to live for You. Thank you for hearing my prayer." In Revelation 3:20 NIV Jesus says, "Here I am! I stand at the door and knock. If anyone hears my voice and opens the door, I will come in and eat with him, and he with me." If you have opened the door of your heart to Him today, He has come in and will be with you forever.

I would love to hear from you. If you have made this decision to turn your life over to God, I would be glad to recommend materials that will help you to grow as a disciple of Jesus Christ. Write me at: jan.edith.taylor@gmail.com

CPSIA information can be obtained
at www.ICGtesting.com
Printed in the USA
LVHW010021220921
698400LV00003B/8